ARIZONA STATE MUSEUM STYLE GUIDE

SECOND EDITION

Compiled by
Carol A. Gifford
and
Carol Ann Heathington

Arizona State Museum
University of Arizona

1989

Archaeological Series 180

ARIZONA STATE MUSEUM

CONTENTS

FIGURES

PREFACE

The Arizona State Museum Style Guide has been developed as an editorial tool and production aid for anthropological and archaeological publications issued by the Arizona State Museum, University of Arizona. Over the past several years, manuscript production has greatly increased and the production technologies have changed dramatically. With the acquisition of word processors and computers, typesetters are often eliminated from the publishing process, and of necessity authors, editors, and typists carry a more direct responsibility for style consistency. In order to assure clarity in scientific reporting and to eliminate confusion for the reader arising from inconsistencies in terminology, the focus of this Guide is on the vocabulary and nomenclature used in the discipline of anthropology.

Many of the features of this manual are designed to save time and space, particularly in terms of the constraints imposed by the typewriter and minicomputer. Of equal importance is the appearance of the typed page. Therefore, the instructions in this Guide represent a compromise between what is feasible and what produces an attractive and easily read page. For example, it may be possible to save the maximum amount of space in references to the literature by eliminating the space between the colon after the date and the page number. To do so, however, produces an inelegant sequence of numbers and punctuation that is relieved by preserving that one space. Despite the growing trend toward eliminating the space, we do not believe any significant amount of paper is saved by deleting it. In material issued by the Arizona State Museum the space is left in, and we strongly advocate a more general return to this practice.

The rules outlined in this Guide, based primarily on *The Chicago Manual of Style*, 13th edition, revised (University of Chicago Press 1982), are to be followed as closely as possible for all publications from the Arizona State Museum, including the *Arizona State Museum Archaeological Series* and the *Anthropological Papers of the University of Arizona*. Appropriate pages in *The Chicago Manual* (1982) are listed for further reference. When unusual material in a manuscript requires style decisions not covered herein, writers and typists are urged to confer with the editor of the series in which publication is expected. We recommend *Webster's Third New International Dictionary* as the final authority on questions of spelling and a recent edition of *Webster's New Collegiate Dictionary* for common spelling. Specific usage of English terms and phrases should follow *A Dictionary of American-English Usage: Based on Fowler's Modern English Usage* (Nicholson 1957).

The most important consideration we wish to impart to those using this Guide is stated in the Preface to *A Manual of Style* (1969): "in all instances" we "advocate the simple and economical in place of the elaborate and expensive," and by so doing we believe that we serve the reader better.

Acknowledgements

This style guide has a lengthy chronological history and genealogy of its own. During 1979 and 1980, Arizona State Museum personnel involved in publishing (Gayle Hartmann, John Robertson, Raymond H. Thompson, and Gwinn Vivian) spent a number of long sessions reviewing an old style guide that was prepared in 1972 by William Robinson and Bruce Harrill for use in editing *The Kiva*. Between 1972 and 1980, that early guide was revised by Hartmann and used for Museum publications. Vivian extracted relevant material from the transcribed tapes of the 1980 sessions and prepared a draft for a new style guide. Meanwhile, the editor of *American Antiquity* circulated a "Style Guide for *American Antiquity*" (1979). Much of that material duplicated instructions in the Museum draft, and we made an effort to keep discrepancies between the two guides to a minimum. The decision to use a computer for manuscript production occurred about this same time, and Keith Kintigh, then with the ASM, was asked to assist in the final preparation of the Guide to ensure consistency with any special requirements of the computer. The final product, distributed by the Museum in 1981, benefited from the efforts of all involved, and contributions were listed in the acknowledgments of that edition.

After several years of experience with the Guide, we recognized the need for further refinements, and Raymond H. Thompson, R. Gwinn Vivian, Carol Ann Heathington, and

Lynn S. Teague of the ASM, and Carol A. Gifford of the Department of Anthropology are mainly responsible for this revised edition. In an effort to broaden the usefulness of the Guide, we have eliminated from the 1981 version the section on format, a topic best handled internally by individual organizations based on the requirements of their own publications and typesetting equipment. In its place is "Guidelines for Authors," covering the author's responsibilities to the editor and publisher and describing how certain tasks in the production of manuscripts are to be performed. Chapter 2 on Manuscript Style remains essentially the same, with additional specific recommendations. Guidelines for reference citations and compiling lists of references are now in Chapter 3. Some changes have been made in the style of reference listings. Several appendixes have been added to assist authors with preferred spelling of plant, animal, and shell species and with metric and temperature conversions so that consistency among the many authors of project reports may be achieved without undue loss of time and accuracy. Additions and corrections have been made to Appendix E to make it a more useful tool for quick reference. Also toward that end, the normal order of references and appendixes has been reversed so that these lists appear together at the back of the book and Appendix E serves as an index to the contents of the Guide.

We especially thank Sue Ruiz for typing this 1988 edition on the computer and for her continued interest in matters of format and consistency. She has produced a typescript version of the Guide as an example of how finished typewritten reports are to be prepared by Museum personnel. Lynn Teague wrote portions of the "Guidelines for Authors." William Robinson and Bruce Harrill, and other editors of *The Kiva* who may recognize portions of their original style guide in this fourth generation, are thanked. Finally, the advice and thorough editing knowledge of Raymond H. Thompson have been freely and extensively used throughout this Guide.

Carol A. Gifford
Carol Ann Heathington

Chapter 1

GUIDELINES FOR AUTHORS

Publications of high quality are achieved through the careful attention of both authors and publishers to the responsibilities of their individual roles. It is therefore in the best interest of authors that materials submitted be complete, meet basic requirements of clarity and format, and reflect their own best efforts with respect to the quality of the manuscript contents. The purpose of this style guide is to assist the author in the preparation of manuscripts that achieve these objectives.

There are two tendencies followed by archaeological writers that frequently lead to unclear scientific expression. One is misplacing modifiers when structuring sentences, a problem discussed by Fowler (1965: 659–661) as unattached participles. The other is attributing human qualities to inanimate objects and situations. These deviations from normal English are so prevalent, especially in site reports, that they have acquired the guise of an "acceptable archaeological language." Editors are urged to be alert for these literary misconstructions and authors are encouraged to make every effort to write exactly what it is they intend to say.

1.1. Manuscript Submission and Review

A manuscript submitted to the Arizona State Museum (ASM) for publication in the *Archaeological Series* should include a clean typescript of all text, a table of contents with a list of figures and tables, copies of all figures and tables, and a complete list of references. Authors are expected to adhere to the style presented in subsequent sections of this Guide. Any intentional deviation from these recommendations must be brought to the attention of the editor at the time of submission.

Material submitted for publication should be clearly written. Accurate communication is best achieved through simple, direct statements written in standard language rather than specialized professional jargon. Concise presentations also communicate better than do lengthy and repetitive discussions. In many cases graphic devices such as figures and tables provide information with greater clarity and brevity than does text.

Unsolicited manuscripts will be considered for publication, but priority is given to manuscripts prepared in compliance with ASM job requirements or fulfilling ASM institutional responsibilities. In every case, if a manuscript is deemed suitable for Museum publication, some form of review precedes a determination of the conditions under which the manuscript may be accepted. It is especially important that reviewers, editors, and publishers be able to proceed in these determinations knowing that the material represents the final effort of the author, exclusive of subsequent responses to review comments and to editorial questions. The author, therefore, must ensure that the manuscript is accurate and reflects the full intention of the author with respect to content and organization.

After a manuscript has been reviewed, it is the responsibility of the author to respond as fully as possible to comments regarded by the editor as warranting revisions. It is expected that the author and the editor will be able to arrive at a mutually satisfactory final product. The author of an unsolicited manuscript may withdraw the manuscript if differences persist. The author of a manuscript completed in the course of ASM job requirements, however, cannot unilaterally withdraw the manuscript. Subsequent resolution of continuing disagreements is subject to policies and procedures established by the conditions of employment.

1.2. Authorship Credit and Acknowledgments

1.2.1. Authorship credit. Authorship should reflect the relative contributions of the participants in the preparation of the manuscript. Individuals must be credited as authors for writing any significant portion of a manuscript. For reports written while the authors are employed by the Arizona State Museum, authorship may be shared with those designing and directing research and those who substantially revise inadequate drafts. Project directors, however, may not assume exclusive authorship by virtue of their positions or as a result of minor revision by them of material written by others. In reports with multiple authors, the individual who provided the intellectual leadership for the project, who was responsible for the design and direction of the report, and who coordinated the production of the manuscript may be designated as Editor, with other contributors receiving authorship credit for individual chapters or sections of the report. The following paragraphs indicate the ways credit may be recognized.

The editor of an ongoing monograph series is not listed on the cover or title page.

The editor of a series of related volumes is listed on the cover and title page as editor.

The editor of a volume containing articles or chapters by other authors is listed as editor on the cover and title page.

Authors and coauthors of monographs are so listed on the cover and title page, either with a senior author listed first, followed by the coauthors listed according to their relative contributions or alphabetically if there are many who made equal contributions. Authors may be designated in the contents and on the first page of individual chapters. When a volume is jointly written by several authors, credit of authorship for chapters or sections is not specified.

The author of a chapter in a multiauthored volume may be listed as an author on the cover and title page and in the contents, or may be listed as a contributor in a volume that has an editor. The term contributor is primarily useful when many authors write several different sections of the volume. "Contributions by . . . " on the cover and title page usually refers to separate chapters, sections, or appendixes by those authors. If there are several authors contributing equally to the volume, normally their names are listed alphabetically.

The author of an appendix may be listed as a contributor, may be mentioned in the acknowledgments, or, more rarely, may be listed as an author depending on the length and the significance of the writing.

Contributors who provide substantial information but do not write lengthy portions of the manuscript do not receive author credit but must be mentioned in the acknowledgments, with a precise description of the nature and extent of their contributions.

1.2.2. Acknowledgments. Proper credit must be given in the acknowledgments for all support given to the project or publication: financial, institutional, and intellectual. It is customary to cite financial aid first, and grant numbers from federal or other agencies are included. Nonfinancial support from institutions such as work space and access to collections is also acknowledged. Contributions from people providing professional expertise and writing small sections of the report that are not listed elsewhere are thanked next, describing their work concisely. Colleagues who took the time to read the manuscript and to offer useful comments on rough drafts normally are included. Brief mention may be made of personal support but a simple statement of the facts without emotional overtones is desirable when acknowledging the support of close associates.

The acknowledgments may be placed at the end of the preface or, if there is no preface, in a separate section (Sec. 1.3.1).

1.3. Manuscript Subdivisions

As indicated in *The Chicago Manual* (1982), a book or monograph usually consists of three major divisions: the front matter, the text, and the back matter. It is the responsibility of the senior author or the editor to submit manuscripts that conform to the following sequence of parts.

1.3.1. Front matter (*The Chicago Manual*, pp. 5–21). Front matter provides information on the content and nature of the work. It normally includes title page, contents (including figures and tables), foreword, preface and acknowledgments, and abstract if used, in that order. Title pages for the ASM *Archaeological Series* are standardized. Other manuscripts may require special title page formats; consult the editor. Reference to the Arizona State Museum on the title page must recognize that it is a division of the University of Arizona:

Arizona State Museum
University of Arizona

The foreword is a statement by someone other than the author, and that person's name appears at the end of the foreword placed flush right. The preface is the author's own statement. Usually acknowledgments are incorporated at the end of the preface, or take the place of the preface if there is none. Other front matter such as dedication, epigraph, and introduction are rarely used in Museum manuscripts but are fully described with examples in *The Chicago Manual*. All front matter parts start on a new page with the title centered and that page is numbered at the bottom with lower case roman numerals.

1.3.2. Text (*The Chicago Manual*, pp. 21–28). The text follows front matter and contains the bulk of information to be conveyed to the reader. Most textual material is divided into chapters. Chapter titles are short whenever possible and should communicate concisely chapter content. Chapters always start on a new page. Every effort should be made to start a chapter on a recto (right-side) or odd-numbered page. When text is printed on both sides of the paper, a chapter may start on a verso page if space is tight or at a premium. The editor or typist should try to adjust spacing or illustrations to avoid both blank verso pages and verso chapter beginnings.

1.3.3. Back matter (*The Chicago Manual*, pp. 28–30). Back matter provides reference material and may include appendixes, notes, glossary, references, and index. When there is more than one appendix, each is given a title and designated by capital letters (for example, Appendix A, Appendix B; *see* Section 1.5.1 for numbering figures in appendixes). Page format follows that used for text.

Most studies include bibliographic information only for the sources used by the author, and the list of these citations is titled References (Sec. 3.2). A bibliography is a list of all known sources of information on a given subject; few manuscripts provide such a complete listing.

All scientific monographs should contain an index, and authors are responsible for compiling it; consult *The Chicago Manual* (pp. 511–557) for rules on indexing. A separate pamphlet entitled "Indexes, Reprinted from A Manual of Style, Twelfth Edition" has been issued by the University of Chicago Press.

1.4. Quotations, References, and Notes

> Quoting other writers and citing the places where their words are to be found are by now such common practices that it is pardonable to look upon the habit as natural, not to say instinctive. It is of course nothing of the kind, but a very sophisticated act, peculiar to a civilization that uses printed books, believes in evidence, and makes a point of assigning credit or blame in a detailed, verifiable way (Barzun and Graff 1977: 262).

It is always the responsibility of the author to submit only original work in which use of material prepared by others is properly acknowledged, cited, and authorized. In cases requiring permission to use or republish material from other sources, a statement documenting that the author has obtained this permission should be submitted with the manuscript and recorded in the acknowledgments or in figure legends. Both quotations substantiating an argument and endnotes expanding on text should not be used indiscriminately. They are devices to be used sparingly and only when necessary to give the reader a fuller comprehension of the subject.

1.4.1. Quotations and references (*The Chicago Manual*, pp. 281–302). Authors should take careful note of the two spellings of archaeology (archeology) and copy quotations and references exactly at the time the manuscript is being written. Preferred spelling in the *Archaeological Series* is "archaeology." The "ae" form is preferred by most American universities and the Society for American Archaeology. The *American Anthropologist* and the U.S. government, notably the Smithsonian Institution and the National Park Service, use "archeology."

All quotations must quote the source precisely, word for word, copying all internal punctuation and accent marks. It cannot be overemphasized that this is the author's responsibility. Each word must be spelled exactly as it is listed in the quoted source. *The Chicago Manual* (p. 283) indicates that "in a passage quoted from a modern book, journal, or newspaper an obvious typographical error may be silently corrected, but in a passage from an older work or from a manuscript source any idiosyncrasy of spelling should be preserved." A spelling error in the original quotation or a word whose meaning appears to be inappropriate to the author's intent may be noted by the insertion of sic (italicized) in brackets to let the reader know that the cited material faithfully represents the original source and that the author or editor is aware of the deviation from modern practice. Generally [*sic*] is unnecessary and should not be overused.

If it is appropriate to delete some portion of a quotation, use ellipses (three dots in the middle of a sentence, four dots at the end of a sentence). Ellipsis points are seldom necessary before a quoted passage, but if used, three precede the quotation. Like [*sic*], ellipses should not be overused. They should never be used in such a way as to distort the author's original intention.

Quotations of less than five typewritten lines are enclosed in double quotation marks and included in the running text. The reference citation may precede the quotation, as in the following paragraph, or author and citation may appear after the closing quotation marks but before the period.

Quotations of five or more lines are single spaced in the final publication. According to *The Chicago Manual* (p. 290):

> Material set off from the text as a block quotation is not enclosed in quotation marks. Any quoted matter within a block quotation should be enclosed in double quotation marks, even if the source quoted uses single marks. Therefore, when a quotation run into the text in the typescript is converted into a block quotation by author or editor, the initial and final quotation marks must be deleted and the internal marks changed . . . . Similarly, if a quotation set off from the text in the typescript is run into the text by the author or the editor, initial and final quotation marks must be added and any internal quotation marks changed accordingly.

Block quotations are indented four spaces from the left margin and four spaces from the right margin. If an extended quotation includes two or more paragraphs, the new paragraph is indicated by an additional four-space indentation of the first line and a blank line is left between paragraphs of a quotation. Extended quotations are followed by a single blank line, and text may resume flush left or begin a new paragraph as appropriate.

1.4.2. Notes (*The Chicago Manual*, pp. 405–420). Notes of any kind are seldom used in anthropological publications. Notes are not used for citation of bibliographic references, and they should not ordinarily be used to include additional material designed to explicate the text. If the material in the note is not essential, then it should be deleted from the manuscript. Notes are not to be used to demonstrate to the reader the author's wide-ranging control of arcane and irrelevant, though interesting, bits of information. Moreover, notes are cumbersome and costly in both typing and printing, and some computers used for producing camera-ready copy cannot print the superscript numbers required for identifying notes in the text.

Occasionally notes are essential accompaniments of ethnographic or historical manuscripts. In such cases, notes may be placed at the back of the book, at the end of a chapter, or at the end of an article. Material so presented is called an endnote. If endnotes are contemplated, agreement must be reached between author and editor concerning their use. Endnotes are numbered consecutively throughout a chapter or article and the number should be placed at the end of a sentence (after the closing punctuation) in superscript. The numbered notes appear at the end of the article or book before the list of references.

Proper numbering in the text and consistency with the numbered listing at the end of the text are the author's responsibility. Any additions to or deletions of notes require renumbering all other notes in both the text and the end listing, and any cross-referencing to notes may have to be revised. These changes are also the author's responsibility.

Footnotes are not used in ASM publications.

1.5. Figures and Tables

A manuscript consists of three classes of material: running text, figures, and tables. Figures include all forms of illustration: photography, line drawing, map, chart, chronological diagram, reproduced form, or other graphic device. The practice of isolating photographic illustrations in a separate section of the monograph, perhaps with its own numbering system apart from other illustrations, was an adaptation to the problems of printing technology of an earlier time. Technological advances in the printing industry have eliminated these problems; photographs are treated like any other illustrative material and are integrated into a single series of illustrations. The term "plate" is not used by the ASM.

Illustrations and tables are always the most expensive part of any publication. Illustrations, therefore, must be chosen with care and with full respect for their importance to the understanding of the manuscript. Each illustration must have a direct and referenced relevance to a part of the text matter. If a potential illustration or table does not (1) help clarify the text, (2) expand on the text, or (3) make possible more abbreviated text, serious questions should be raised as to why it should be included. Illustrations are not decorative devices, nor are they a modern parallel to the illuminations in medieval manuscripts. Their purpose is not to provide visual relief from unending pages of dull text, but rather to enlighten and inform the reader on the subject of the study.

1.5.1. Figures (*The Chicago Manual*, pp. 303–320). Figures should be constructed in a size and shape suitable for the publication in which they are to appear. Every effort should be made to have illustrative material run vertically on the page. Figures that must appear horizontally always face right, whether bound as a verso or a recto page. Authors or volume editors are required to provide all illustrations in final usable form, with photographs and line drawings of high quality. Letter and line width on figures and maps should be adequately proportioned for future reduction; thick letters often blur when reduced. Lettering on illustrations should not be typewritten. The use of stick-on lettering may cause problems in the production process. Some adhesives, such as rubber cement and those used on stick-on lettering, may separate in the dry desert air, causing the loss of portions of illustrations prior to printing. Authors should confer with the editor or the press production department prior to making final versions of figures or illustrative material.

A metric scale for illustrated objects must be available to the reader; consult the editor for preferred methods. The height, length, rim diameter, or maximum diameter of the largest item in the figure may be given in the legend, identified by its letter (for example, rim diameter of *a* is 10.2 cm, or length of *c* is 6.8 cm). For some publications the editor may require that a metric rule be included in the figure itself. Designations in the caption such as ½ scale cannot be used because the author does not know what size the illustration will be in the final publication, and reductions by the printer will distort the scale. When a key is necessary to explain symbols used on a map or drawing, it is best to place it within the boundaries of the figure. Keep the symbols and the explanation in the key of sufficient size to accommodate reduction of the figure. A long list of site names, keyed to the map by number, is more appropriate in the legend.

Map symbols follow the normal conventions for longitude and latitude designations and with regard to contour, river, state, or international boundary lines. These conventions are shown in Figures 1.1 and 1.2. Always included are a north arrow, a metric scale on the map, and, for area maps covering a small region, an inset placing the map location in a wider geographic context.

Labeling on maps should be horizontal as often as possible. Diagonal labels may read either bottom to top (for a low left to high right slant) or top to bottom (for a high left to low right slant), but consistency throughout is preferable on a single map. Do not label rivers, for instance, in such a way that the printing, part way through the name, reverses direction. In all cases, care must be taken to avoid having any part of the wording appear to be upside down on the page. Letter size should vary according to the significance of the feature being labeled. All-one-size lettering on a map is confusing and makes it difficult to comprehend the purpose of the map. It is the author's responsibility, especially when figures are drawn by others, to check all spelling and the position of words prior to submitting the final figures to the editor or press.

Figures are numbered consecutively within each chapter. The illustrations in Chapter 1 are numbered 1.1, 1.2, 1.3; those in Chapter 2 are 2.1, 2.2, 2.3. In appendixes, which are identified by letters, figures are numbered A.1, A.2 (Appendix A) or B.1, B.2 (Appendix B).

Figures have a caption or short title, often followed by a longer legend when needed for clarity. The caption is placed beneath the illustration with figure spelled out, for example:

> *Figure 1.1.* Pottery from Site 3: *a*, bowl of Fourmile Polychrome; *b*, sherds of Fourmile Black-on-red; *c*, sherds of Cedar Creek Polychrome. (Rim diameter of *a* is 20 cm.)

Captions end with a period or, when followed by a legend, by a colon (preferably) or a period (with long complex legends) and two spaces, followed directly by the legend (the legend does not start a new line). Short *a, b, c* items are separated by semicolons (preferred style); in legends containing longer material or complete sentences, use periods between items. Normally captions and legends are typed flush left for all lines, both first and runover lines. Do not center short runover lines, but short one-line captions may be centered beneath the figure. Caption and legend appear under the bottom of the figure and face the same way as the figure. Usually captions do not extend beyond the edges of illustrations.

The caption or short title is listed in the contents under "Figures," but explanatory material in legends is not included. Captions should be as brief as possible, but clearly inform the reader of the general content of the illustration.

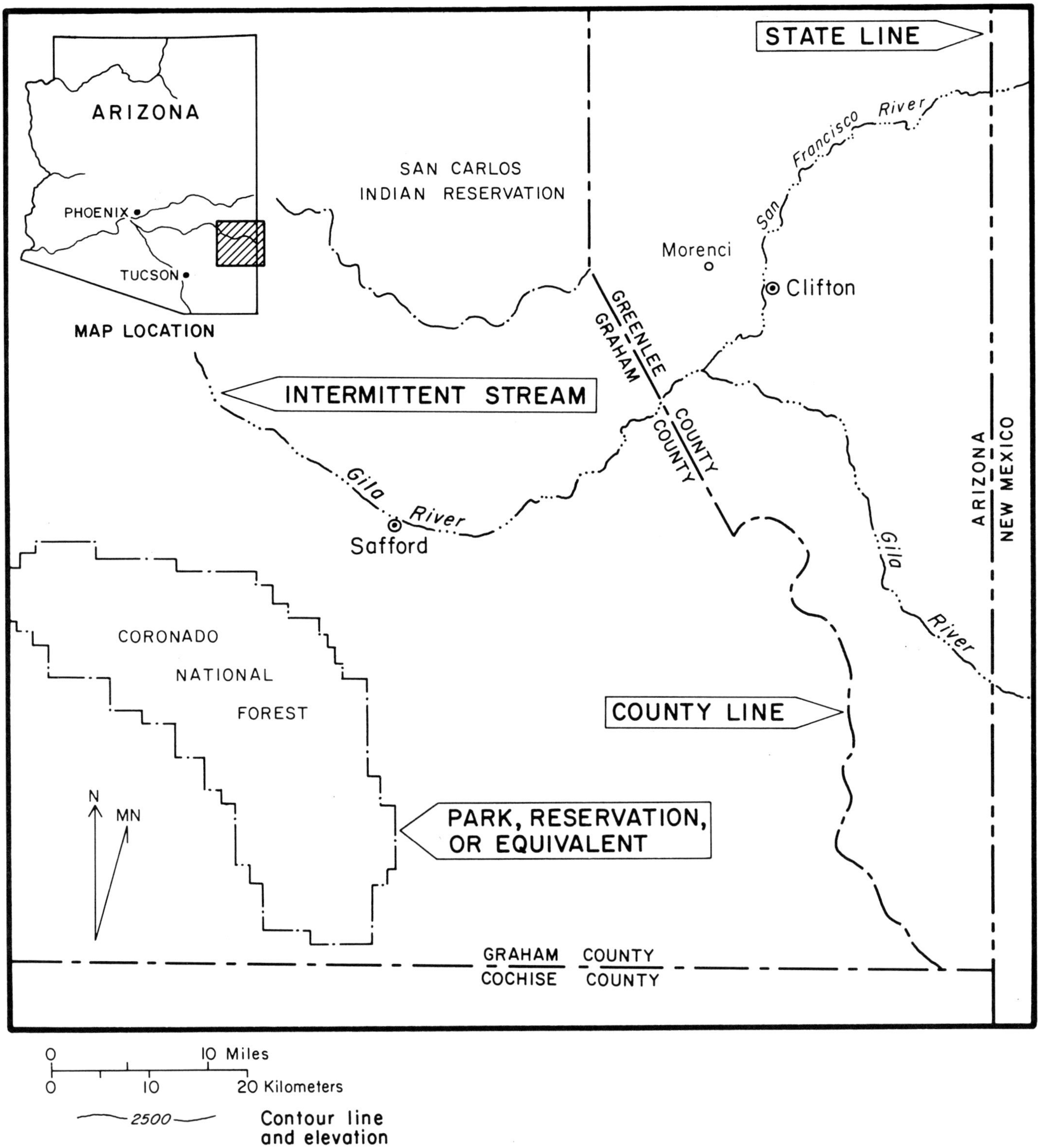

Figure 1.1. Conventional symbols used on maps.

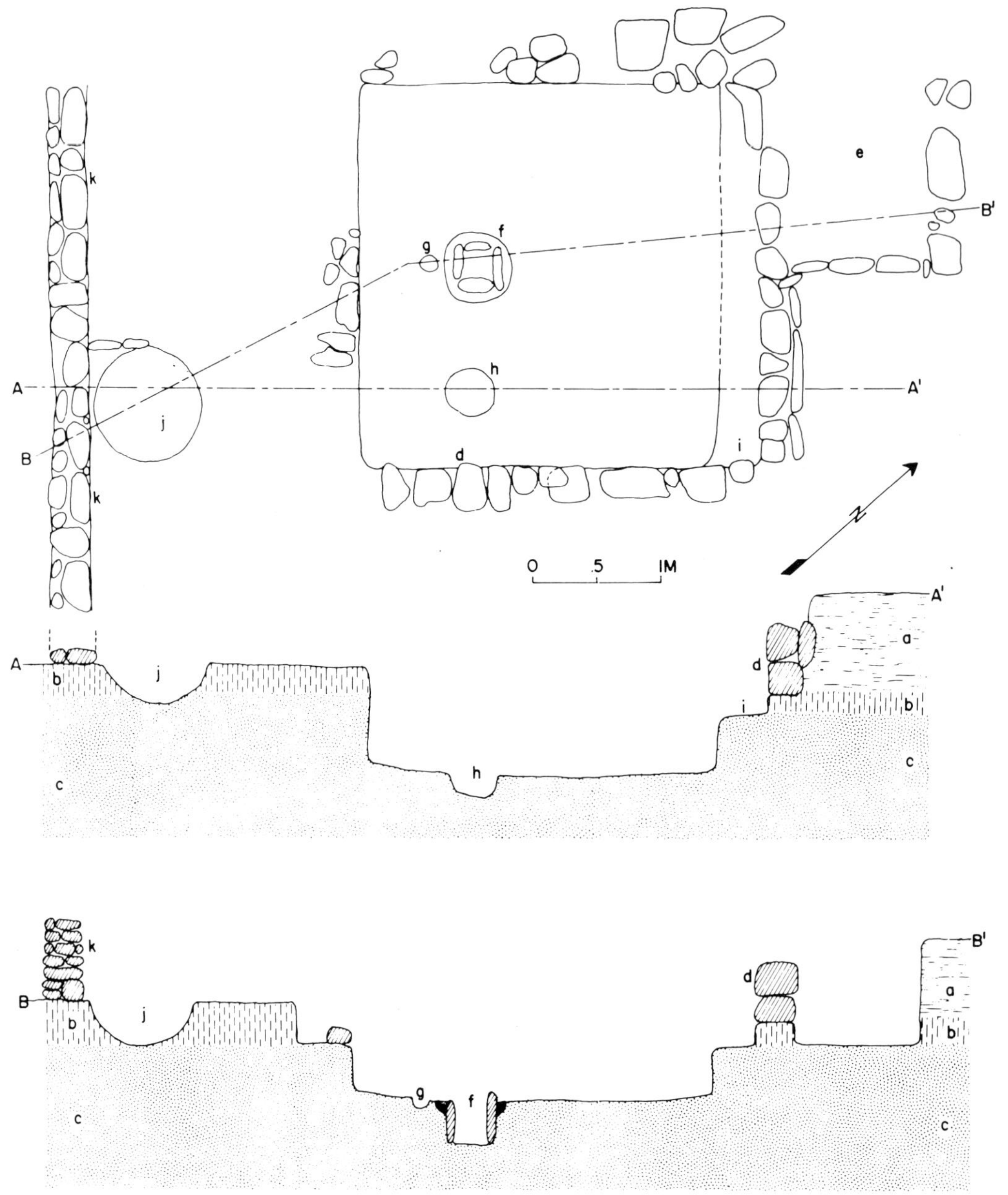

Figure 13. Plan and sections of Unit Structure 2: *a*, silt and refuse; *b*, black clay; *c*, yellow sandy silt; *d*, roughly laid masonry; *e*, annex structure; *f*, slab-lined hearth in clay hearth; *g*, floor pit; *h*, sand-filled pit; *i*, bench; *j*, large firepit; *k*, wing wall.

Figure 1.2. Example of site plan and section drawings. (Figure reproduced from *Mogollon Culture in the Forestdale Valley, East Central Arizona*, by Emil W. Haury, 1985, with permission of the University of Arizona Press, Tucson.)

All figures must be cited in the text. When mentioned in the body of a sentence, "Figure" is spelled out; when cited in parentheses, it is abbreviated (for example, Fig. 3).

1.5.2. Tables (*The Chicago Manual*, pp. 321–350). Although tables are convenient for displaying data in a single place, they are expensive to type and print. The author should consult the editor before tables are typed in final form. The editor has the authority to reorganize tables in consultation with the author. Complex tables and lists of data such as artifact counts and measurements should be placed in an appendix. Tables that appear in the text are intended to clarify the discussion or provide the reader with a quick overview of the subject. Such tables are designed to summarize the data rather than itemize them.

A table is a two-dimensional device for displaying information that normally arranges data on two axes. Tables with more than two axes usually confuse the data rather than display them for easy access. Most lists of information (other than simple enumeration of related items that form an integral part of the running text) can be presented as tables. Whenever possible, a long table should be divided into a number of more interpretive short ones. A two-page table should appear on facing pages (if the report is printed on both sides of the paper), with the top identifying column headings repeated on the second page.

Tables are arranged vertically on a page whenever possible. Horizontal tables always face to the right, whether bound as a verso or a recto page, and on verso pages, an adequate margin must be left at the bottom of the table for binding. Table number and title are centered at the top of the table. A single reference or source can be placed in parentheses beneath the table title. If notes are necessary, they are indicated in the table either by superscript small numbers or letters or by superscript symbols arranged numerically or alphabetically from left to right going from top to bottom throughout the table.

Every effort must be made to avoid confusion when numbers are placed in the cells formed by the columns and rows of a table. Columns of numbers should be positioned so that the decimal points (and commas) are aligned. In long distribution tables it is common practice to indicate only occurrences without attempting to distinguish between lack of occurrence and lack of data. In small and analytical tables it may be necessary to make such a distinction, in which case a zero is often used to indicate no occurrence and a blank cell to indicate that no data are available. Dashes are not used in the cells of tables. A column or row that includes only one or two entries should be redesigned by accommodating the limited entries in a note at the bottom of the table.

Tables, like figures, must be cited in the text. Tables are numbered consecutively within chapters: Table 1.1, Table 1.2 in Chapter 1; Table 2.1, Table 2.2 in Chapter 2; Table A.1 in Appendix A. Examples of various kinds of tables are presented in Figures 1.3 and 1.4.

1.6. Proofreading (*The Chicago Manual*, pp. 90–105).

Both editors and authors should proofread final typescripts or proofs, performing somewhat different functions. The author's responsibility involves substantive matters concerned with the correctness of specialized terms and the accuracy of tables. The editor is responsible for typographic and stylistic accuracy. When the author is unavailable to perform this duty promptly, the publication schedule may require that all proofreading be done by the editor.

In all cases, corrections in final typescripts or galley proofs must be held to a minimum. The editor has the final authority regarding any changes. Sometimes the only changes that can be made are those that correct grievous errors or that avoid serious misinterpretations of the meaning of the text.

All authors and typists should be familiar with the proofreader's marks in Figure 1.5. Editors and authors are expected to follow these conventions in marking manuscripts and typists should be able to accurately retype edited material in accordance with these designations.

TABLE 14.3

Bifaces

Field Number	*Length (mm)*	*Width (mm)*	*Thickness (mm)*	*Material Type*	*Feature Number*
141	63.9	26.4	8.4	Quartzite	33
143	47.9	26.5	6.4	Chert	33
528	35.9*	37.7	7.8	Chert	33
529	36.5	33.4	7.4	Quartzite	33
3098	136.0	56.5	10.2	Chert	113
3100	90.6	40.6	11.5	Quartzite	113

* Fragmentary

TABLE 9.23

Mean Vessel Dimensions (in mm) by Surface Finish, Vessel Form, and Site

Surface Finish Variant	*Dimension*	*Martinez Hill*		*San Xavier*		*Hodges*	
		Bowls	Jars	Bowls	Jars	Bowls	Jars
Red-on-brown	Body diameter	223.29	203.85	220.00	246.50	257.14	247.43
	Vessel height	86.14	188.25	115.86	187.75	139.19	216.57
Smudged	Body diameter	394.00	—	280.33	—	244.84	—
	Vessel height	143.50	—	103.50	—	136.11	—
Slipped	Body diameter	142.50	154.50	174.00	212.00	253.00	—
	Vessel height	105.00	140.00	137.00	182.00	—	—
Site Collection	Body diameter	212.00	185.27	199.67	235.00	266.00	224.00
	Vessel height	98.33	181.36	117.45	185.83	138.07	207.22

TABLE 9.10

Motifs in the Secondary Design Field, All Vessels

Motif	*Number of Occurrences*
Straight line or band*	23
Triangle	33
Diamond	4
Parallel lines or bands*	8
Zigzag line	6
Rectangle	2
Rectilinear scroll	14
Total	90

* Bordered and unbordered variants; otherwise bordered only

TABLE 9.22

Student's T-Tests for Vessel Dimensions Comparing Vessel Form (Bowls vs. Jars) by Site

Site	*Body Diameter*			*Vessel Height*		
	t	p	df	t	p	df
Martinez Hill	1.07	>0.10	25	-6.52	<0.001	24
San Xavier	-0.18	>0.90	16	-3.57	<0.001	15
Hodges	-0.73	>0.20	49	-3.96	<0.001	49

t = Student's t-value
p = Probability
df = Degrees of freedom

Figure 1.3. Examples of table formats used in the *Arizona State Museum Archaeological Series* (from Number 171).

Table 4.3 Radiocarbon Dates from Materials Associated with Sulphur Spring Stage Artifacts

Site	Unit	Laboratory Number	Material dated	Date (yr B.P.)
Arizona FF:6:9	Db	A-3233	Charcoal	8,390 ± 190
		A-3230	Charcoal	8,500 ± 180
	Da	A-3231	Charcoal	8,420 ± 180
		A-3232	Charcoal	8,650 ± 180
		A-3314	Humates	8,860 ± 160
Arizona FF:6:8	Db	A-3237	Charcoal	8,140 ± 220
		A-3238	Charcoal	9,340 ± 180
	Da			No dates
Arizona FF:10:1	Db[1]	A-3377	Charcoal	8,840 ± 310
		A-3379	Charcoal	8,760 ± 210
		A-3378	Humates	8,970 ± 220
	Da[2]			No dates
Arizona FF:10:14	Dc			No dates
Lehner site, Arizona		SMU-197	Charcoal	9,860 ± 80
		SMU-204	Charcoal	9,900 ± 80

1. Ten additional radiocarbon dates range from 8,000 yr B.P. to 9,340 yr B.P. for unit Db at Arizona FF:10:1, but their source material was not directly associated with artifacts (see Table 2.1).
2. Two radiocarbon dates on charcoal of 10,420 ± 100 yr B.P. (A-1152) and 8,920 ± 1150 yr B.P. (Tx-1199) were obtained from unit Da 240 m downstream from Arizona FF:10:1, but the charcoal was not directly associated with artifacts (see Table 2.1).

Table 7.2. Residence of Descendants

	Percentage of Descendants				
		Residing in Mexico, by Town Population			
Town of Ancestral Origin	Remaining in Ancestral Town	Below 5,000	5,000–50,000	Over 50,000	Residing in the United States
San Juan (N = 114)	75[a]	4	2	16	4
Paricutin (N = 25)	48[b]	12	4	36	0
Angahuan (N = 24)	71	0	25[c]	4	0
Zirosto[d] (N = 87)	60	2	7	17	14
Zacan (N = 42)	36	10	2	50	2
All Towns	62	4	6	22	6

a. In new location, San Juan Nuevo Parangaricutiro.
b. In new location, Caltzontzin.
c. Descendants of Paracho woman who married an Angahuan man. All in Paracho.
d. Includes those in Old Zirosto, nearby New Zirosto (Rancho Baranca Seca), and in the refugee settlement, Miguel Silva.

Table 5.1. Population Distribution in the Valley of Sonora

Valley Area And Phase	Floodplain-oriented Houses N	Floodplain-oriented Houses %	Arroyo-oriented Houses N	Arroyo-oriented Houses %	Total Houses N	Total Houses %
Northern						
Early phase	66	29.5	19	8.4	85	37.9
Late phase	763	59.2	68	5.3	831	64.5
Southern						
Early phase	127	56.7	12	5.4	139	62.1
Late phase	437	33.9	21	1.6	458	35.5
Valley Total						
Early phase	193	86.2	31	13.8	224	100.0
Late phase	1,200	93.1	89	6.9	1,289	100.0

Each relic house is used as a surrogate for a household averaging 6.1 persons.

Table 4.1. Classification of Pottery in the Bladen Ceramic Complex (Group frequency based on 1302 rim sherds)

Ware	Group	Type	Variety
Unspecified	Copetilla (2.2%)	Copetilla Unslipped	Gallon Jug Variety
Rio Nuevo Glossy	Consejo (55.6%)	Consejo Red	Estrella Variety
		Barquedier Grooved-incised	Barquedier Variety
		Fireburn Red-and-cream	Fireburn Variety
		Fireburn Red-and-cream	Unnamed Variety
		Cudjoe Composite	Cudjoe Variety
		Cudjoe Composite	Unnamed Variety
		Other Consejo Ceramic Group	Unspecified (1 modeled, 1 fingernail incised, 1 punctated, 2 black-on-red)
	Machaca (1.6%)	Machaca Black	Wamil Variety
		Chacalte Incised	Yo Creek Variety
	Quamina (1.3%)	Quamina Cream	Quamina Variety
		Tower Hill Red-on-cream	Tower Hill Variety
		Tower Hill Red-on-cream	Unnamed Variety (resist)
		Other Quamina Ceramic Group	Unspecified (1 gadrooned, 2 grooved-incised, 3 fine-line incised)
Fort George Orange	Chicago (24.1%)	Chicago Orange	Nago Bank Variety
		Cotton Tree Incised	Cotton Tree Variety
Unspecified	Honey Camp (15.2%)	Honey Camp Orange-brown	Honey Camp Variety
		Copper Bank Incised	Copper Bank Variety

Figure 1.4. Examples of table formats used in the *Anthropological Papers of the University of Arizona* (4.3 from Number 45, 7.2 from Number 46, 5.1 from Number 48, 4.1 from Number 47).

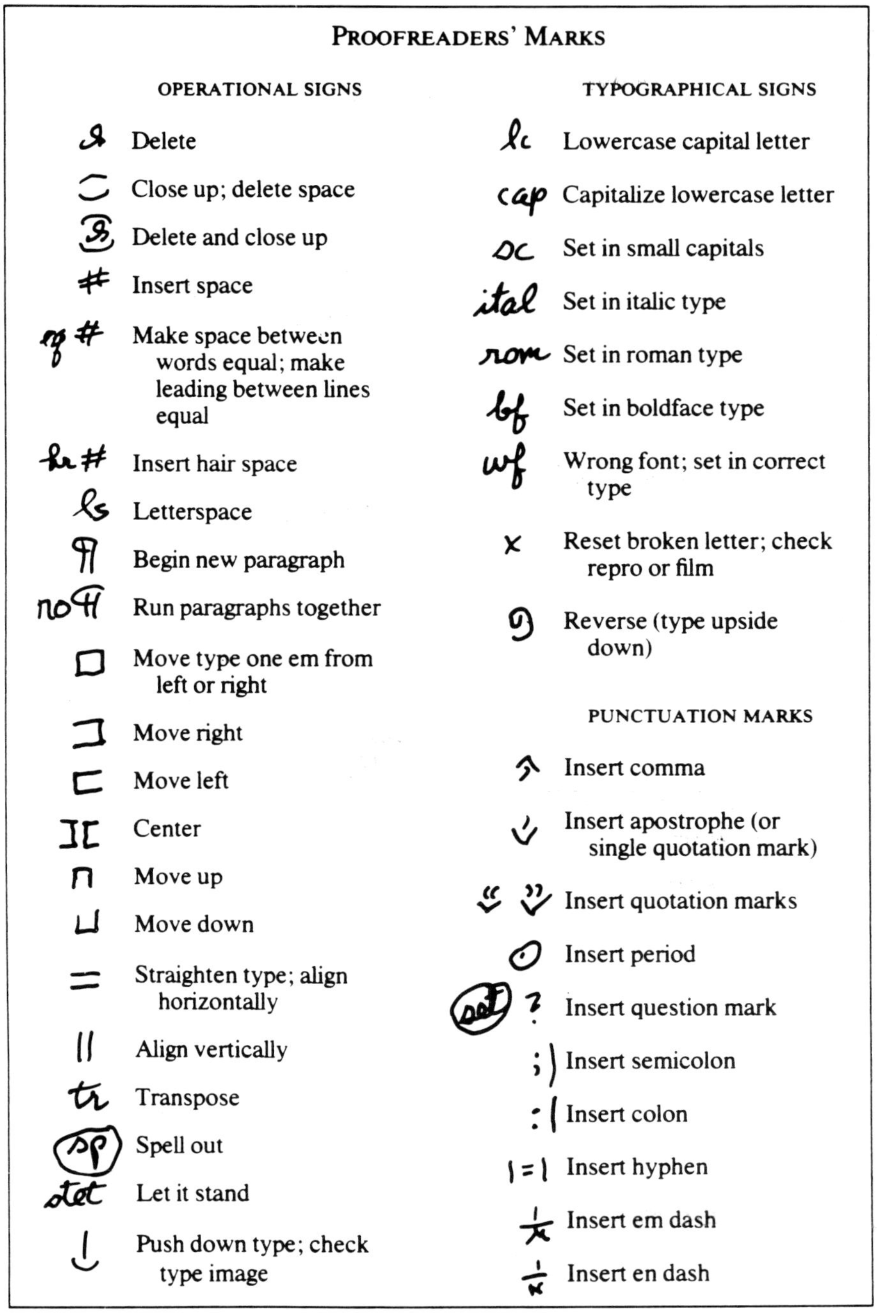

Figure 1.5. Proofreaders' marks. (Reprinted from *The Chicago Manual of Style*, 13th edition, p. 94, with permission of the University of Chicago Press, copyright 1969 and 1982 by the University of Chicago.)

Chapter 2

MANUSCRIPT STYLE

The importance of consistency in manuscript style is elucidated by Mary J. Scroggins, an editor and seminar leader for Editorial Experts, Inc.

> The English language is rich in stylistic and grammatical variations and choices. Consistency dictates that this richness not clutter a piece (and thus interfere with correct communication) by giving the readers an overabundance of choices.
>
> Readers ought to be able to depend on consistency in editorial style, usage, and format for guidance to the writer's intentions and interpretation. Consistency can hold together a less-than-superior piece that has substance, and it can add polish to a really fine piece. . . .
>
> Inconsistency . . . undermines the effectiveness of the manuscript and the credibility of the writer or the project's sponsor. The work is devalued.
>
> Inconsistency can damage and even destroy credibility. . . . If the writer or editor does not take pains with such obvious matters as hyphenation, number style, spelling preference, capitalization, and abbreviations, how can readers be sure that appropriate care was taken with less obvious details such as accuracy of data collected and thoroughness of research? Inconsistency hangs about such a piece of writing like a sign that warns, "Reader Beware."
>
> Inconsistency may also divert readers from the writer's purpose. In the struggle to decipher the puzzle of choices, readers may misinterpret, overlook, or completely ignore important information. If readers must decide whether "site," "facility," and "center" refer to the same location or whether the variable on page 2 is the same as the one on page 10, even though one has a capital *C* and the other has a lowercase *c*, energy that should be used to absorb information must be used to consider the probability of intent.
>
> Clearly, consistency should be imposed by the writer and the editor, never the readers. Consistency indicates the writer's and the editor's common respect for the readers and concern for the importance of correct, expedient communication (Scroggins 1988).

The preferred forms of terms, measurements, and references presented below should be used in all material issued by the Arizona State Museum. They are intended for long-term use and are not to be altered merely to keep in step with the changing styles of particular scientific journals.

2.1. Capitalization

Capitalize names of specific archaeological and geographic areas, proper names of chronological, cultural, and geologic divisions, taxonomic names of generic and higher order, and proper names of archaeological classes. Examples of preferred capitalization of archaeological terms are listed in Appendix E under generalized items such as site, village, complex, and so on. Numbered archaeological features are capitalized (Feature 1; Trench 2; Burial 3; Trenches 3, 5, and 10). For nonarchaeological words follow *The Chicago Manual of Style* (13th edition).

2.1.1. Site names. Both the name of a site and the generic term that follows such as village, pueblo, ruin, or site are capitalized. When two or more sites are named, the generic term is lower case (for example, Arsenic and Tule Tubs caves).

Naco Site
Promontory Village
Grasshopper Pueblo
Hodges Ruin
Ventana Cave
Red Bow Cliff Dwelling
Sudden Shelter

2.1.2. Site numbers. All site numbers in the computerized AZSITE system of the Museum are preceded by the two-letter capitalized abbreviation for the relevant state (for example, AZ for Arizona, NM for New Mexico); these abbreviations follow Postal Service state abbreviations. Site numbers assigned by other institutions should follow the format used by that institution and should include the institutional abbreviation (listed in Vogler 1980: 59). Although the institutional designation need not always be used with ASM AZSITE numbers, it should be used if there is any possibility of confusion. Site numbers in the Gila Pueblo system require spelled-out place names and site number followed by GP.

AZ BB:12:3 ASM
(AZ D:16:4 MNA)
AZ FF:11:1 AMF
(AZ T:12:23 ASU)
Pearce 10:1 GP
(Sonora B:6:1 GP)
NA 3742
LA 847

Arizona site numbers assigned by the National Forest Service read:

FS: AR–03–09–01–01
FS: AR–03–09–01–14

Arizona site numbers assigned by the Bureau of Land Management read:

AZ:AA:16:1 BLM

2.1.3. Cultural and temporal designations (*The Chicago Manual*, p. 204). The cultural name is capitalized, but the generic term that follows is lower case.

Early Man site
Mogollon culture
Anasazi area
Maya region
Hohokam villages
Anasazi tradition
Llano complex
Culiacan horizon
Kayenta district
Basin-and-Range province
Cenozoic era
Pliocene epoch
Cochise culture horizon
Winslow branch
Pioneer period
Sacaton phase
San Pedro stage
a Trincheras site (nonspecific)
Pine Lawn phase sites
Patayan root
Clovis point
Folsom fluted points

By tradition, certain historical periods and some cultural stages recognized by their characteristic technology are capitalized.

Christian Era
Stone Age
Bronze Age

2.1.4. Geographic place names. Both the name of the feature and the generic term are capitalized. If more than one named feature is given, the generic term is lower case. For Arizona place names, see Barnes (1988). Barnes is preferred to Granger's (1982) revised and enlarged version of *Arizona Place Names*, although Granger should be consulted for place names not found in Barnes.

Paiute Mesa
Glen Canyon
Santa Catalina Mountains
San Juan Island
Colorado Plateau
Santa Cruz Valley (name of valley)
Salt River valley (valley used descriptively)
Carrizo Creek
Whitewater Draw
Cow Springs Wash
Nantack Ridge
Colorado River
  Gila and Salt rivers
Tucson Basin
central New Mexico
middle Gila
southwest (direction)
  southwestern Mexico
  southwestern Arizona
Southwest (region)
  Southwestern Indians
  Southwestern pueblos

In anthropology, the Southwest as a region refers to a particular culture area of a portion of the southwestern United States and northwestern Mexico having specific geographic and cultural attributes. When the adjectival term Southwestern is used in the sense of a culture area rather than in a directional sense, the word may be spelled with a capital *S*.

2.1.5. Names of Institutions and Political Divisions (*The Chicago Manual*, pp. 196-203). All parts of the names of institutions, except articles and prepositions, are capitalized (Arizona State Museum, Museum of Northern Arizona). The word Museum, capitalized, may be used after making an initial reference to the Arizona State Museum. The abbreviation ASM may be used if it is introduced in parentheses following the first reference.

Use lower case when referring to federal, state, county, or city governments, unless the reference is made specifically to "the State" or "the City." Capitalize such terms only when they are part of a proper name (for example, the city of Tucson, the state of Arizona, but Pima County).

2.2. Ceramic Terminology

Specific pottery types, wares, and varieties are capitalized and all components of a term are capitalized except in cases of hyphenated descriptive terms. A colon and one space are placed between a type and its variety when both are given.

Do not use abbreviations such as B/W in the text and such abbreviations should be avoided in tables. Do not adjoin the term ware to pottery type names (for example, Alma Plain, not Plainware). By tradition, the secondary compound descriptive terms in Southwestern archaeology are spelled open with the words capitalized, except for phrases like black-on-white or red-on-buff. Examples from the Southwest are listed below.

Alma Plain (not Plainware)
Alma Fingernail Incised
Alma Neck Banded
McDonald Painted Corrugated
Pine Flat Neck Corrugated
Grasshopper Obliterated Corrugated
Point of Pines Indented Corrugated
Mesa Verde Black-on-white (not Black-on-White)
Tusayan Corrugated: Tusayan Variety
Verde Brown Ware
White Mountain Red Ware
Tularosa Fillet Rim
Tanque Verde Red-on-brown
Sacaton Red-on-buff
Gila Polychrome
Mimbres Bold Face Black-on-white

but

Mogollon brown wares
red ware sherds
Hohokam buff wares
Salado polychromes

The compound descriptive terms used in Mesoamerican archaeology appear with hyphens with only the first word capitalized.

Yalbac Smudged-brown
Ixcanrio Orange-polychrome: Ixcanrio Variety
Jato Black-on-gray: Jato Variety
Urita Gouged-incised: Urita Variety
Pabellon Modeled-carved: Pabellon Variety

Define all terms used unless those terms are defined elsewhere as in *Ceramics for the Archaeologist* by Anna O. Shepard (1956) or in *Pottery Analysis, A Sourcebook* by Prudence M. Rice (1987).

2.3. Ethnic Names

Ethnic names are capitalized. When the name refers to a tribe or group, only the singular form is used in a generic sense. The common English addition of an *s* to form a plural is never used for tribal names. The *s* is used with an apostrophe only for the possessive form.

Hopi	It is the Hopi's land
Seri	The Seri are woodcarvers
Pima	He lived among the Pima for years
Tohono O'odham	(formerly Papago)
Navajo	(not Navaho)

When individual members of an ethnic or tribal group are identified, the plural form with an *s* is used (for example, two Hopis passed by or three Navajos were at the trading post).

Adjectival forms of tribal names do not differ from the name itself. Do not use an *n* to form adjectives: a Pima house, not a Piman house. Ethnic names with an *n* added often are used by linguists to identify the language of the ethnic group. The rule presented here for adjectives helps prevent confusion with the linguistic usage (the Piman language).

2.4. Dates (*The Chicago Manual*, pp. 238–240)

A.D. precedes dates, B.C. follows dates (400 B.C. to A.D. 500; the community was inhabited from A.D. 1075 to 1200). A.D. and B.C. are set in small capital letters in typeset copy.

In B.C. dates, the higher number appears first, in A.D. dates, last (1200 to 900 B.C., but A.D. 900 to 1200).

Commas are used only when there are more than four digits in the date (4000 B.C., 10,000 years, 2100 B.C.).

Apostrophes are not used in dates (1920s, not 1920's).

Full entries for inclusive years are used in titles or headings (1945–1960). Inclusive dates in running text normally use the word "from" followed by "to" (from 1945 to 1960, not from 1945–60).

Hyphens are used in dates with prefixes (post-A.D. 1000, mid-1300s).

2.4.1. Radiocarbon ages. The conversion of radiocarbon ages in the years before present to Christian calendric dates must take into account temporal variations in the natural radiocarbon content of the atmospheric carbon dioxide. Klein and others (1982) provide calibration tables with a confidence level of 95 percent in the conversion of a radiocarbon age to a calendric date (Huckell 1983), and the Klein publication should be consulted for calibrated dates. B.P. dates may cause confusion and the author must indicate the base date (representing the "present") used by the laboratory involved. (Among archaeologists, the B.P. present is generally recognized as 1950.) The international symbol B.P. indicates radiocarbon years ago (dates not calibrated); B.C. indicates calendrical dates derived by subtracting 1950 from uncalibrated radiocarbon ages.

Laboratory number follows age and date if age is announced for the first time. If a published reference exists, the citation follows the age and date. One space occurs before and one after the ± symbol and periods are used with B.C. and A.D. designations. Use C-14, not C^{14}.

Radiocarbon age of 11,950 ± 100 years: 10,000 B.C. (Laboratory number).
Age of 950 ± 100 radiocarbon years: A.D. 1000 (citation).

2.4.2. Archaeomagnetic dates. In early practice, archaeomagnetic dates were reported in the same form as C-14 dates, that is, as a mean value plus or minus a certain number of years (A.D. 1015 ± 35). It is now considered more accurate to report dates as ranges, for example, A.D. 980–1050. Both conventions for reporting archaeomagnetic dates continue to be used and when such dates are cited, follow the quotation exactly. For DuBois's dates, use mean value form; for all other dates, use the range form. Unless a symbol font is readily available, it is easier to spell out alpha 95 than to use a symbol. When alpha 95 is used as an adjective, hyphenate: the alpha-95 value.

Remanence is the magnetic induction remaining in a magnetized substance when the magnetizing force has become zero. Thus, use remanent (not remnant) magnetization in studies of archaeomagnetism.

2.5. Measurements (*The Chicago Manual*, pp. 234-235, 391-394)

The metric system of measurements is preferred, although English units of measurement may be used when following the common precedent set for describing artifacts in historic archaeology reports. English measurements should not be abbreviated in running text. It is also appropriate to show both kilometers and miles, with miles in parentheses following kilometers. Elevations should be given in meters (followed by feet in parentheses) above sea level. Measurements in the English system are maintained in quotations or when citing measurements from another author. In these cases, however, the metric equivalent should be given in brackets or parentheses. It is the author's responsibility to provide metric measurements. Some metric conversion tables are in Appendix D.

Metric abbreviations are given when used in combination with Arabic numerals. Metric unit abbreviations are not followed by a period. A space is left between the number and the unit abbreviation. In sequences of numbers, each number should be followed by its unit abbreviation. The abbreviation may be written out in running text if using the abbreviation causes confusion or if it is unclear when typed (for example, one liter rather than 1 l). All measurement units are spelled out when used nonspecifically or at the beginning of a sentence, and square meter is never abbreviated except in a table (the grid units covered 100 square meters). Hyphens are used when a measurement is used as an adjective (10-m intervals). Measurements of range or approximation use the connecting word *to*, not a hyphen (for example, 10 to 15 days or 2 cm to 3 cm deep). Do not use a slash to replace the word *per* in text. Fractions are expressed by decimals with measurements, and decimals of less than one are preceded by a zero (1.5 cm by 0.5 cm).

millimeter	mm	kilogram	kg
centimeter	cm	gram	g
meter	m	liter	l
kilometer	km	centiliter	cl

The excavation area was 3 m by 2 m by 10 m.
The artifacts were found several meters away.
Ten-centimeter levels were established for Locus A.
The pit house measured 3 m by 4 m.
The houses are 3 m, 5 m, and 7 m long.
3 to 15 days
a 1-m by 2-m test pit
3 m to 15 m long
3 to 9 percent (not 3–9 percent)
200 to 300 square meters
13 person-days per site
A distance of 10 km (6.21 miles)

2.6. Numbers (*The Chicago Manual*, pp. 231–247)

For cardinal numbers spell out numbers zero through nine except: in measurements and dimensions (3 cm), in combination with numbers over nine (3 to 15 days), and for numerical designations (Pit House 3, Chapter 5).

Use arabic numbers for numbers greater than nine. Approximate figures in hundreds, thousands, or millions are spelled out (for example, there were hundreds of potsherds). Numbers of four or more digits ordinarily include commas (but do *not* use commas in four-digit dates or addresses).

Spell out ordinal numbers first through ninth; use numbers thereafter (for example, eighth, 10th, 11th).

Spell out all numbers that begin a sentence: Twenty of the burials were flexed. Often it is better to restructure the sentence to avoid beginning with a number, especially when the number is a long one or in hyphenated form.

Familiar, often-used fractions may be spelled out in text (for example, one-half of the vessels, a third of the specimens, three-fourths of the items). Do not use spelled-out fractions with measurements; decimal designations should be used (for example, 1.5 cm by 0.5 cm). Always precede a decimal figure of less than one with a zero.

Township, Range, and Section locations should be clearly specified in the text, and their manner of designation may be determined in part by their quantity in the manuscript. If legal descriptions appear only infrequently, as in establishing the location of a given site or sites, they should be spelled out (Township 12N, Range 13E, Section 36). If, however, they are used throughout a manuscript (as may be the case in survey reports), they may be abbreviated as follows: T12N R13E. The shorter form should be used in tables. Fractions may be used in identifying parts of sections (for example, the NE ¼ of the SW ¼ of Section 10, but shortened versions such as NE ¼ SW ¼ should appear only in tables).

Grid units designated by Cartesian coordinates should be written as follows: N13 E4 or N300–310 E190–200. A single space (not a dash, comma, or slash) separates the coordinates.

For occasional use in running text, spell out centuries such as first century, sixteenth century. If an entire monograph contains many such entries, the editor may use numbers for that specific publication (16th century). When century is used as an adjective in a compound word, hyphenate (nineteenth-century artifacts).

The Arizona State Museum does not use roman numerals in references or in text (except to accommodate scientific designations: Dimension II, Layer IIIB). When citing old references that use roman numerals for volume or plate numbers, change them to arabic numbers. Most dictionaries show the equivalences under the word "number" in a Table of Numbers.

For mathematical and statistical material, follow the rules given in *The Chicago Manual* (pp. 351–373).

2.7. Degrees of Temperature (*The Chicago Manual*, pp. 235, 395)

Degrees are spelled out in ordinary text matter and follow the rules governing the spelling out of numbers (it was twenty degrees colder than when he started climbing). In scientific text abbreviations for Centigrade (C) and Fahrenheit (F) may be used with arabic numerals (10° C). When giving degrees of temperature, give Centigrade followed by Fahrenheit in parentheses. When citing an author who uses degrees Fahrenheit, put the Centigrade conversion in parentheses (or in brackets within a direct quotation) following the Fahrenheit. Appendix D provides temperature conversions.

2.8. Percent (*The Chicago Manual*, p. 235)

The word percent is spelled out and is written as one word. The symbol (%) may be used in parentheses or in tables, and need not be repeated within columns that are labeled Percent or % at the top. Percent may take either a singular or plural verb (40 percent of the lithic assemblage was chipped; 11 percent of the vessels were slipped). When percent occurs with a number in an adjectival phrase, do not hyphenate: at the 95 percent confidence level.

2.9. Scientific and Common Names of Plants and Animals (*The Chicago Manual*, pp.217–218)

When using the Latin scientific term, genus is capitalized, species is not; both are italicized (underlined). According to *The Chicago Manual*, divisions larger than genus (phylum, class, order, and family) are capitalized but do not appear in italics. English derivatives of scientific names are lower case: carnivores (order Carnivora), canids (family Canidae), chenopodium (genus *Chenopodium*). The term cheno-am is an English derivative. When a Latin proper noun is used as a species name, it is written in lower case: *Agave parryi*. Proper nouns in the common name carry normal capitalization: Parry agave.

When the species is unknown and no species of that genus has been identified in the collection or from the site, sp. (abbreviation of species, singular) is used following the genus name. It is also used when the investigator does not know if the genus contains more than one species. When several species occur in the genus or when several species have been identified in the collection or from the site, but it is impossible to assign a particular specimen to one of these species, spp. (abbreviation of species, plural) is used.

Pinus ponderosa (genus and species); ponderosa pine
Artiodactyla (order); artiodactyl (English derivative)
Glycymeris shell (genus)
Three glycymeris (English derivative) bracelets were in the burial.
Olivella shell (genus); a string of olivella (English derivative) beads
Cercidium-Cereus community (general)
Canis spp. (several species of Canidae present, but species of this particular fragment unidentifiable)

When using cf., meaning to compare further with a specific species, be sure to include the genus initial, capitalized.

Odocoileus hemionus (mule deer)
Odocoileus virginianus (white tail deer)
Odocoileus cf. *O. virginianus*

Lists of plants, animals, and shells frequently recovered from Southwestern sites, including scientific and common names, are presented in Appendixes A, B, and C.

"Sources of Information" following Chapter 3 contains a listing of the standard references to be consulted for proper spelling and capitalization of technical terms.

2.10. Abbreviations (*The Chicago Manual*, pp. 375–398)

Latin abbreviations are not used in Museum manuscripts. Instead substitute the whole-word English equivalents. Never use ibid, op. cit., or loc. cit.

English equivalents of common Latin abbreviations are:

cf.	confer, compare (may be used in taxonomy, not with references)
ca.	about
e.g.	for example
et al.	and others
etc.	and so forth
et seq.	as follows
i.e.	that is

In some material it may be permissible to use abbreviations for institutions after the institution has been spelled out in the text (for example, ASM; check with the editor). In most instances, it is appropriate to refer to the Arizona State Museum as the Museum; however, if multiple institutions are mentioned, use ASM. The abbreviation should appear in parentheses following the name when it is first used, for example, Gila Pueblo (GP), Arizona State Museum (ASM), Museum of Northern Arizona (MNA).

Metric measurements are abbreviated when used with numbers (for example, 8 mm, 0.5 cm; *see* Section 2.5). For abbreviations of species (sp., spp.) in Latin names, *see* Section 2.9.

2.11. Accents and Other Diacritical Marks

Accents, tildes, and other diacritical marks must appear if they are used in a foreign language. On word processors and when setting type, it is usually easier to use English equivalents when they exist (pinyon, for example, rather than piñon).

2.12. Italics

Generic, specific, or varietal names of plants and animals and titles of books, journals, poems, and other literary works should appear in italics in the text. *See* Chapter 3 for the use of italics in the list of referencs.

2.12.1. Foreign words (*The Chicago Manual*, pp. 169–171). *The Chicago Manual* (pp. 169, 171) indicates that

> Isolated words and phrases in a foreign language may be set in italics if they are likely to be unfamiliar to readers . . . . In deciding whether or not to italicize, the author's and editor's task is to place the word on the spectrum of usage stretching from foreign-and-unfamiliar at one end to unforeign-and-familiar at the other. And for doing this there are no guides but sensitivity and common sense.

Foreign words in common use and listed in a recent edition of *Webster's New Collegiate Dictionary* do not appear in italics (for example, in situ, a priori, barranca, barrio). In the middle range are words in the process of becoming incorporated into English. These words should appear in italics the first time they are used in the text (exactly as spelled in the foreign language, with diacriticals), followed by a definition of the term. Thereafter such words appear in roman type. Examples are *ranchería, pochteca, ak chin*. Totally unfamiliar foreign words must also be defined when first used, but should remain in italics throughout the text. It is best to rephrase sentences than to use foreign words extensively throughout the text.

2.13. Compound Words (*The Chicago Manual*, pp. 162–164, 176–181)

Consult *The Chicago Manual* (Table 6.1) for a thorough discussion of compound words. In general, if the word does not appear in *Webster's New Collegiate Dictionary* as one word (either a closed or hyphenated compound), spell it as two words (open compound word). Certain common archaeological compound words have been spelled extensively in the literature as one word; see Appendix E for these exceptions. Similarly, hyphens are no longer used in some descriptive phrases that would normally require them. Compound adjectives are generally hyphenated when they precede the noun; nouns and modifiers following nouns are not hyphenated (for example, the clay-lined firepit, the firepit was clay lined; the alpha-95 value). The common practice of creating long descriptive phrases by converting several nouns into adjectives should be avoided, if possible. In no case should such a phrase itself be converted into an adjective, for this inelegant construction would require a long string of hyphens. Restructuring the sentence always will result in greater clarity.

Words formed with prefixes (such as post, pre, non, sub, semi) are not strictly compounds and are therefore not hyphenated. Except in special situations all words formed with prefixes are spelled closed. According to *The Chicago Manual* (p. 180), those special situations include the following.

1. When the second element is a capitalized word or a numeral (un-American, post-1941). Although certain commonly used archaeological terms are now spelled solid with the capital letter moved to the prefix (for example, Precolumbian, Preclassic Maya), many others are not (for example, pre-Hispanic, pre-Basketmaker, pre-Classic in the Southwest).
2. When there is a need to distinguish homonyms (re-cover, re-create).
3. When the second element is more than one word (non-English-speaking people, pre–Civil War).

Compound words formed with the suffix *-like* are spelled closed (floorlike) except those formed from proper names (Mexico-like), words ending in *l* (sail-like), and word combinations (pre-Basketmaker-like).

For common tree and plant names, traditional spellings (generally open compounds) are preferred. For example, bear grass, brittle bush, bur sage, cat claw, creosote bush, palo verde, and rabbit brush are spelled as two words with no hyphen. Consult *Trees and Shrubs of the Arizona Desert* by Benson and Darrow (1981). Many species recovered from archaeological contexts in southern and central Arizona are not included in that book and a good second source for plant names is *A Catalogue of the Flora of Arizona* by Lehr (1978). A list of commonly used plant species and the preferred spellings of their common names is provided in Appendix A.

2.14. Preferred Spelling of Foreign and Frequently Used Words

The preferred dictionary for spelling is *Webster's Third New International Dictionary of the English Language, Unabridged*. A recent edition of *Webster's New Collegiate Dictionary* may be used for common words.

When words in Spanish, Native American languages, or other languages are used, the word should be spelled as it is in that language. Accents, tildes, and other diacritics must appear if used in the original language. If the word appears in *Webster's,* it is *not* italicized (not underlined; for example, barrio).

Some words that have become "loan words" in English or have been modified to fit English orthography may be used. Consult the list below and Appendix E, or check with the editor for accepted spelling. These loan words need not be italicized in the text. Foreign words that are not common should be italicized when first used (Sec. 2.12.1). If the word appears extensively in the manuscript it does not have to be italicized throughout the manuscript, although it must be spelled correctly with diacritical marks.

Archaeology must be spelled with the *aeo* instead of the *eo* in all cases except in quotations, excerpts, or reference titles, which must follow that author's spelling. The journal *American Anthropologist* and publications from government agencies such as the National Park Service and the Smithsonian Institution use *eo.*

Preferred spellings of some frequently used words are as follows:

appendixes
barranca
barrio
eolian
gray
Navajo
palo verde
Papaguería
pinyon
pochteca
ranchería
saguaro
sherd
Zuni

2.15. Commonly Misused Words

Short, precise words should be used rather than their longer forms: use (not utilize), begin (not commence). Use methods, not methodology, in describing procedures followed (for example, "Excavation methods are outlined below"). Methodology refers to the full range of methods and procedures used by a discipline. Form and morphology are not synonymous, and the latter is normally used in a biological sense. Several words or sets of words are often misused by many writers and clarifications for some of these are given below.

2.15.1. That and which. These two common words serve many purposes and are frequently confused. The following distinctions provide a guide for dealing with the most common confusion. In grammatical terms, *that* is used with a restrictive clause, *which* is used with a nonrestrictive clause that is set off by commas. The information after *that* is basic to the point being made; the information after *which* is almost (but not quite) parenthetical.

> The sherd that was found in the fill was part of a jar rim. (In this sentence the location is important.)
>
> The sherd, which was found in the fill, was part of a jar rim. (Here the emphasis is more on what the sherd was than where it was found.)

2.15.2. Since and because. It is preferable to use *since* when conveying a sense of time and *because* when meaning "in view of the fact that."

2.15.3. While and whereas. *While* is used only as an adverb of time. In other contexts, *although* or *whereas* should be used.

2.15.4. And/or. In *The Careful Writer*, Bernstein (1978) advises:

> Whatever its uses in legal or commercial English, this combination [and/or] is a visual and mental monstrosity that should be avoided in other kinds of writing. Fortunately it is almost always unnecessary. . . . For instance: "The law allows a $25 fine and/or thirty days in jail." The solution here is to write out in plain English, at the cost of just one extra word, what the and/or means: "$25 fine or thirty days in jail or both."

2.15.5. Fewer and less. In general, use *less* for quantity and *fewer* for number; for example, the building has less floor space than the Empire State, yet it contains no fewer than 1,200 offices.

2.15.6. Affect and effect. *Effect* as a noun means "result" (for example, the effects of this process may be seen in . . .); as a verb, it means "to bring about," "to accomplish" (for example, to effect a change in the Museum's policy on . . .). *Affect* is a verb meaning "to influence" (for example, many factors affect site distribution).

2.15.7. Farther and further. *Farther* refers to distance (for example, he chased the ball farther). *Further* refers to time or quantity (for example, he pursued the subject further).

2.15.8. Variation and variability. *Variation* is the "act or process of varying, the state or fact of being varied, an instance of varying, the extent to which or range in which a thing varies." *Variability* is "the state or quality of being variable."

2.15.9. Singular and plural forms. Some nouns that describe or refer to more than one item are singular and take singular verbs; variety and total are two such words (for example, the variety of beads on that one strand was unique; a total of 378 lithic artifacts was found). As a pronoun, *none* takes a singular or plural verb, depending on the subject to which it refers. The word *percent* also may take a singular or plural verb, depending on how it is used in the sentence.

The following words form the plural with *-a*, *-ia*, or *-i*. Care should be taken to use these words correctly, and to use the proper verb form (for example, data are or were).

singular	*plural*
cactus	cacti
colloquium	colloquia
criterion	criteria
datum	data
focus	foci
locus	loci
phenomenon	phenomena
stratum	strata
symposium	symposia

Chapter 3

CITING AND LISTING REFERENCES

The purpose of references is to document for the reader the sources of information used. Do not cite anything that is not available to the reader or not needed to develop the ideas presented in the monograph. In addition to published material, other sources including manuscripts, letters, maps, and field notes that are available at a public repository (for example, library or museum archives) may be cited, but a manuscript in the possession of the author is unacceptable.

Always provide the most specific information possible. For example, do not cite Teague and Crown (volume editors) when referring to Fish's discussion of Hohokam agriculture in the example below.

Fish, Suzanne K.
1984 Agriculture and Subsistence Implications of the Salt-Gila Aqueduct Project Pollen Analysis. In "Hohokam Archaeology along the Salt-Gila Aqueduct, Central Arizona Project: Environment and Subsistence," edited by Lynn S. Teague and Patricia L. Crown. *Arizona State Museum Archaeological Series* 150(7): 111–138. Tucson: University of Arizona.

Do not cite one author as cited by another if the original reference is available. Such second-hand references are only acceptable when it is impossible to consult the original reference.

3.1. Reference Citations in the Text

Reference citations in the text follow the author-date system. The author's name may appear in the body of a sentence followed by the date in parentheses, or both the author's name and the date may be placed within the parentheses.

Recent investigations by Smith (1966) have produced new data.
Recent investigations in the area (Smith 1966) have produced new data.

The term *author* in these examples includes (in addition to authors) volume editors, compilers, assemblers, and other individuals responsible for organizing the book or monograph cited.

3.1.1. Format of author-date citations

One author
Robinson (1972)

Two authors
Robinson and Harrill (1975)

More than two authors
Robinson and others (1977)

In rare cases, there may be more than one cited work that would be abbreviated the same way. Both of the examples below would ordinarily be abbreviated as Fish and others 1985.

Fish, Suzanne K., Paul R. Fish, and John Madsen
1985 A Preliminary Analysis of Hohokam Settlement and Agriculture in the Northern Tucson Basin. In "Proceedings of the 1983 Hohokam Symposium, Part I," edited by Alfred E. Dittert, Jr. and Donald E. Dove. *Arizona Archaeological Society Occasional Paper* 2: 75–100. Phoenix: Phoenix Chapter, Arizona Archaeological Society.

Fish, Suzanne K., Paul R. Fish, Charles Miksicek, and John Madsen
1985 Prehistoric Agave Cultivation in Southern Arizona. *Desert Plants* 7(2): 107–112.

If both publications are cited, each must be clearly identified in the text, and the author and editor should agree on the best method of doing so. The simplest method is to use all the authors' names (especially for publications with three authors), but in other instances (four or more authors or different subjects) another solution may be preferred. Several methods of clearly identifying these publications are outlined in *The Chicago Manual* (p. 402). The shortest and clearest way is by listing all authors.

(Fish, Fish, and Madsen 1985)
(Fish, Fish, Miksicek, and Madsen 1985)

One author, several references
Robinson (1968, 1972, 1977)

Multiple references in one year for an author (or multiple authors) are arranged alphabetically by title (ignoring A, The, El, Los) in the list of references at the end of the book, *not* sequentially according to their appearance in the text (for example, 1968a does not need to appear in the text before 1968b). Editors should check the list of references for this a, b, c ordering before editing the manuscript.

One author, several references in the same year
Robinson (1968a, 1968b); do not use (1968a, b)

" . . . The order in which multiple references are cited is determined by the author who cites them. Editorial rearranging in alphabetical or chronological order without consultation with the author is not recommended" (*The Chicago Manual*, p. 404).

Several authors cited in one place
(Robinson 1968; Smith 1977; Harrill 1980)
Robinson (1968), Smith (1977), and Harrill (1980)

Two authors with same last name

In rare cases, works written by authors with the same last name and published in the same year may be cited. If so, the first initial (or very rarely, two initials) of both authors must be used throughout the report to distinguish these publications.

McGuire, Randall H.
1980 The Mesoamerican Connection in the American Southwest. *The Kiva* 46(1–2): 3–38.
McGuire, Thomas R.
1980 Mixed-Bloods, Apaches, and Cattlebarons: Documents for a History of the Livestock Economy on the White Mountain Reservation, Arizona. *Arizona State Museum Archaeological Series* 142. Tucson: University of Arizona.

These must be cited in the text as (R. McGuire 1980) and (T. McGuire 1980) respectively.

Sometimes it is necessary to use middle names, for example:

Paul Schultz Martin (the palynologist)
Paul Sydney Martin (the archaeologist)

No author specified

If no author's name appears on the title page, cite the sponsoring agency or publisher (Sec. 3.2.11).

(World Trade Bureau 1972)
(Commission on Indian Affairs 1916)

3.1.2. Citations of specific pages. Do not use p. or pp. as page abbreviations following the year of publication; the colon replaces them and it is understood that the numbers that follow refer to pages. Preferred style for material originating in the Museum is to leave one space following the colon after the date.

Robinson (1972: 6) or (Robinson 1972: 6)
Robinson (1972: 17–21)
Robinson and Harrill (1975: 35)
Robinson and others (1977: 270)
Robinson and others (1977: 181–187)

Discontinuous page references are listed sequentially.

Robinson (1972: 13, 22, 29)
Harrill (1977: 23–27, 34)

Typists should be aware that the date and page number are typed closed in material being prepared for *American Antiquity* or the *American Anthropologist* (for example, 1972:6).

3.1.3. In Press citations. *In Press* means that the work is actually in production and listed by the publisher. When used, the citation should read: (Robinson, in press). Do not use *In Preparation*. If the manuscript is not actually in the hands of the publisher, it may be cited as a manuscript on file (Sec. 3.2.10) if it is available, or referred to in the text as a source of information (Sec. 3.1.4).

3.1.4. Personal communications. Personal communication references are never used. Generally two situations create what has been perceived as a need for references to personal communication. The first is a highly specific personal communication that is relevant to what is being stated in the text. In these cases the format of the sentence should be changed to include the reference. In keeping with the purpose of references, try to provide the reader with as much information as possible. For example, "Fragments similar to these were found by Lisa Huckell in her recent analysis of flotation samples collected from Corona de Tucson project (ASM) sites in the northern Santa Rita Mountains." Although lengthy, such a citation provides the reader with information on: (1) who is the source of the information, (2) the geographic area in question, and (3) the project and the institution sponsoring the work. This information is especially important as a clue to publications that may be forthcoming. The second situation involves cases where many items of information that are relevant to the monograph or book have been provided by an individual; in these instances acknowledgment of this individual's contribution should be given in the preface or acknowledgments.

3.1.5. Figures, tables, and plates in citations. Care must be taken to be sure there is no confusion between references to illustrations and tables in cited material and to those in the text itself. If the reference appears in a sentence without parentheses, figure, table, and plate are spelled out and capitalized; if it appears in parentheses, figure is abbreviated. When the year of publication is followed by a figure, table, or plate designation, a comma follows the year; a colon is used only to replace p. or pp. The page number is not given when the figure, table, or plate can be identified by its number. When the figure, table, or plate is listed along with page numbers, page numbers normally appear first, followed by a comma. When citing old publications, the title used for the illustrative material (figure, map, plate, graph, chart, table) must be used, but roman numerals should be converted to arabic numbers.

> Jones (1932, Fig. 3) illustrates . . .
> (Jones 1932: 217, 310, Plate 9)
> (Haury 1977, Table 98)
> (Mallery 1893, Plate 12), not XII

3.2. List of References

3.2.1. Arrangement of references. All references cited in the text must appear in the references and all entries in the references must be cited in the text. References are arranged in alphabetical order by the author's last name. The author's first name, not the initial, is to be used in the list of references. Two or more works by one author are listed chronologically by date of publication. Two or more works by one author published in the same year are differentiated by lower case letters following the date of publication; these a, b, c entries are arranged alphabetically by title (Sec. 3.1.1). References with more than one author are arranged numerically by the number of authors (two authors before three authors, and so on) and alphabetically by succeeding authors within the numerical categories.

> Willey, Gordon R.
> Willey, Gordon R., and William R. Bullard, Jr.
> Willey, Gordon R., and Philip Phillips
> Willey, Gordon R., William R. Bullard, Jr., and John B. Glass
> Willey, Gordon R., T. Patrick Culbert, and R. E. W. Adams
> Willey, Gordon R., William R. Bullard, Jr., John B. Glass, and James C. Gifford
> Willey, Gordon R., A. Ledyard Smith, William R. Bullard, Jr., and John A. Graham

The names of Latin American authors are frequently alphabetized incorrectly. In most cases, the surname has two parts, for example, Robles Ortiz, or even Robles O. The name Manuel Robles Ortiz is alphabetized as Robles Ortiz, not as Ortiz.

When the text includes a quotation that contains a cited quote within it, the writer should provide both citations in the references. Authors should obtain the full reference from the source itself *at the time they are using the citation* to avoid time-consuming rechecking later. Do not use lists of references in other works as a source of bibliographic information because this procedure tends to perpetuate errors.

3.2.2. Books and chapters or articles in books. The words in titles are capitalized with the exception of articles and prepositions not appearing as the first word. A book title is italicized or underlined (both words and intervening spaces may be underlined). Chapter titles and titles of articles in edited books are neither in italics nor quotation marks (see Schoenwetter and Dittert below). Place of publication and publisher must be shown for books, monographs, or series, but not for journals because the place of publication for journals frequently changes. In those rare instances where the state must be included with the place of publication it is written out, not abbreviated (for example, Portland, Maine, to distinguish it from Portland, Oregon). Place of publication is listed first, followed by a colon, one space, and the publisher. If two publishers' names appear on the title page, both are listed. It is not necessary to include "Inc.," "Publishing Company," and similar information. "Washington" is sufficient for material published in Washington, D.C., by the Government Printing Office. The reference entry ends with a period. For books in foreign languages, see *The Chicago Manual*, 13th edition, pp. 448–449.

These general rules are illustrated in the examples that follow. Exceptions to these rules are noted in Sections 3.2.3 through 3.2.11.

> One author
> Jennings, Jesse D.
> 1968 *Prehistory of North America*. New York: McGraw-Hill.

> Multiple authors
> Binford, Sally R., and Lewis R. Binford
> 1968 *New Perspectives in Archaeology*. Chicago: Aldine.

> Edited book
> Spicer, Edward H., editor
> 1961 *Perspectives in American Indian Culture Change*. Chicago: University of Chicago Press.

> Article in edited book
> Schoenwetter, James, and Alfred E. Dittert, Jr.
> 1968 An Ecological Interpretation of Anasazi Settlement Patterns. In *Anthropological Archaeology in the Americas*, edited by Betty J. Meggers, pp. 41–66. Washington: Anthropological Society of Washington.

3.2.3. Series and monographs. The words in the name of a series and the title of a monograph appearing in the series are capitalized (with the exception of articles and prepositions not appearing as the first word), and the name of the series is in italics (underlined). The title of the monograph is neither in italics nor in quotation marks. The series number follows the series name with no punctuation, but the number is not in italics. The part or issue number is given in parentheses adjacent to (with no space) the series number (see Judd below). Page references follow the series or volume number, separated by a colon and one space. Whenever page references deal with an item within a volume or a volume in a series that does not include a number (see Stephenson below), the abbreviation pp. is used rather than a colon. When an article is in an edited monograph or volume that is published in a series, the words of the article title are capitalized, but the title does *not* appear in quotation marks. The words of the volume or monograph title are capitalized and the title is enclosed in quotation marks following the word "In" (see Rouse below).

Volume in a series

Adams, William Y., Alexander J. Lindsay, Jr., and Christy G. Turner II
1961 Survey and Excavations in Lower Glen Canyon 1952–1958. *Museum of Northern Arizona Bulletin* 36, *Glen Canyon Series* 3. Flagstaff: Museum of Northern Arizona.

Breternitz, David A.
1960 Excavations of Three Sites in the Verde Valley, Arizona. *Museum of Northern Arizona Bulletin* 34. Flagstaff: Museum of Northern Arizona.

Gladwin, Winifred, and Harold S. Gladwin
1935 The Eastern Range of the Red-on-buff Culture. *Medallion Papers* 16. Globe, Arizona: Gila Pueblo.

Hammond, George P., and Agapito Rey
1956 The Rediscovery of New Mexico: 1580–1594. *Coronado Cuarto Centennial Publications (1540–1940)*, Vol. 3. Albuquerque: University of New Mexico Press.

Judd, Neil M.
1964 The Architecture of Pueblo Bonito. *Smithsonian Miscellaneous Collections* 147(1). Washington: Smithsonian Institution.

Office of Indian Affairs
1912 Primitive Agriculture of the Indians. *Office of Indian Affairs Bulletin* 1. Washington.

Stevenson, Matilda C.
1894 The Sia. *Eleventh Annual Report of the Bureau of American Ethnology*, pp. 3–157. Washington: Smithsonian Institution.

Article in an edited or multiauthor volume in a series

Rouse, Irving
1958 The Inference of Migrations from Anthropological Evidence. In "Migrations in New World Culture History," edited by Raymond H. Thompson. *University of Arizona Bulletin* 29(2), *Social Science Bulletin* 27: 63–68. Tucson: University of Arizona.

Tagg, Martin D., and Bruce B. Huckell
1984 The Sycamore Canyon Sites. In "Miscellaneous Archaeological Studies in the ANAMAX-Rosemont Land Exchange Area," by Martyn D. Tagg, Richard G. Ervin, and Bruce B. Huckell. *Arizona State Museum Archaeological Series* 147(4): 61–106. Tucson: University of Arizona.

3.2.4. Journal articles. The words in the titles of journal articles are capitalized, with the exception of articles and prepositions not appearing as the first word. Titles of journal articles are not italicized or enclosed in quotation marks. The journal name is italicized (underlined). The issue number must be included in parentheses immediately following the volume number, for example, *American Antiquity* 46(1): 93–112. Many journals do not carry page numbers on the spine or cover, and without the issue number, finding the appropriate reference is made more difficult and time consuming. Page numbers for articles in journals should list all digits (for example, 154–169, 1454–1455). Place of publication and publisher are not shown.

Longacre, William A.
1964 Archeology as Anthropology: A Case Study. *Science* 144(3625): 1454–1455.

Olson, Alan P.
1966 A Mass Secondary Burial from Northern Arizona. *American Antiquity* 31(6): 822–826.

Royal Society Conference of Editors
1968 Metrication in Scientific Journals. *American Scientist* 56: 159–164.

Ungnade, Herbert E.
1963 Archaeological Finds in the Sangre de Cristo Mountains of New Mexico. *El Palacio* 70(4): 15–20.

3.2.5. Magazine articles. Magazine articles frequently carry a by-line and when the number of contributors is large, the first author may be listed followed by: "and the staff of (name of magazine)," or whatever designation is used by the magazine. The entry continues with the year, title of the article, magazine name in italics (underlined), issue date, and page.

Gibson, John R., with the magazine's international bureaus
1981 After the Summit, a Time of Testing. *U.S. News and World Report*, July 27: 25–28.

If it is impossible to determine the author, treat the reference as an anonymous document (Sec. 3.2.11).

3.2.6. Paper presented at a meeting. Papers presented at professional meetings are treated as is other unpublished material and should be cited only if a copy is available in a public repository for the reader to consult. The words of the title are capitalized, but are not in italics or quotation marks.

Wasley, William W.
1966 Classic Period Hohokam. Paper presented at the 31st Annual Meeting of the Society for American Archaeology, Reno. MS, Arizona State Museum Library, University of Arizona, Tucson.

3.2.7. Dissertations and theses. Several universities do not have dissertations published through University Microfilms.

These and master's theses are treated as unpublished works; their titles are capitalized but not italicized (not underlined). Titles of dissertations published by University Microfilms are italicized (underlined). The words "doctoral" and "master's" are preferred over the abbreviated Ph.D. and M.A.

Reid, J. Jefferson
1973 *Growth and Response to Stress at Grasshopper Pueblo, Arizona*. Doctoral dissertation, University of Arizona, Tucson. Ann Arbor: University Microfilms.

Roberts, Frank H. H., Jr.
1927 The Ceramic Sequence in Chaco Canyon, New Mexico and Its Relation to the Cultures of the San Juan Basin. MS, doctoral dissertation, Department of Anthropology, Harvard University, Cambridge.

Maurer, Michael D.
1970 Cibecue Polychrome, a Fourteenth-Century Ceramic Type from East-Central Arizona. MS, master's thesis, Department of Anthropology, University of Arizona, Tucson.

3.2.8. In press references. A reference cited as in press must not only be accepted by the publisher but be far enough into production that an anticipated date of appearance is known. Works that do not meet these criteria are listed as unpublished manuscripts (Sec. 3.2.10). In press may be written on one line, with the following title further indented, or it may be written on two lines.

Haury, Emil W.
In press Point of Pines, Arizona. A History of the University of Arizona Archaeological Field School. *Anthropological Papers of the University of Arizona* 50. Tucson: University of Arizona Press.

3.2.9 Published material without a date (*The Chicago Manual*, p. 460). "When there is no ascertainable date of publication in a printed book, 'n.d.' (no date) takes the place of the date in the facts of publication. When the date is ascertainable, but not printed in the book, it is enclosed in brackets."

3.2.10. Unpublished material with or without a date. Do not cite an unpublished manuscript unless it is available for consultation in some public repository. A manuscript in the possession of the author is not acceptable. The purpose of listing an item in the references is to enable the reader to consult the author's sources. If you have the only copy of a manuscript and wish to cite it, you must first submit a copy to the Arizona State Museum Library or some other public repository. Do not place copies of another author's work in a library or other repository without the author's permission.

Letters are not permitted as cited references unless the letter is in the Arizona State Museum Archives or a similar location where it can be obtained. Letters should not be cited as personal communications (Sec. 3.1.4).

References used from the ASM Archives should include the name of the document, name of the collection, and manuscript or record group number.

Haury, Emil
1936 Gila Pueblo Collection, MS 15. Emil Haury to J.O. Brew, 4 March. Arizona State Museum Archives, University of Arizona, Tucson.

An unpublished manuscript, like a dissertation or thesis, is listed by author. Words in the title are capitalized, and the year in which the manuscript was written is used as the date. The abbreviation "n.d." (no date) may be used for old material for which the date is not known if it is inappropriate to estimate the date of writing. It is better to show a range of years for the probable time of production of the manuscript such as [1920–1927] or to indicate the likely, though uncertain, year such as [1905?] than to use n.d.

Brandes, Raymond S.
1956 An Archaeological Survey within Gila County, Arizona. MS, Arizona State Museum Library, University of Arizona, Tucson.

Schroeder, Albert H.
1965 Ecological and Cultural Factors and Some of Their Effects on the Southwestern Indian Farmers in Historic Times. MS of INQUA Meeting, Arizona State Museum Library, University of Arizona, Tucson.

United States Weather Service
1924–1927 U.S. Weather Service records on file at Mesa Verde National Park, Colorado.

3.2.11. Author unknown. An anonymous document is usually treated as if the sponsoring body were the author.

United Nations
1962 *Report of the United Nations Scientific Committee on the Effects of Atomic Radiation*. General Assembly, Official Records: Thirteenth Session, Supplement 17 (A/3838).

The citation in the text would read (United Nations 1962). This rule also applies to articles in magazines when the author is unknown (*U.S. News and World Report* 1980), and if several references to the magazine are made for the same year, the a, b, c entries are listed alphabetically by title.

If both the author and source of an anonymous work are unknown, the publication is listed by its title; do not use Anonymous in place of the author's name. Date and publishing information follow on the next line of the reference.

3.3. Arizona State Museum Computerized Master Bibliography

The master bibliography is a cumulative set of computerized bibliographic entries composed of references commonly cited in the Museum's *Archaeological Series*. Most of the entries are publications dealing with Southwestern (especially Hohokam) archaeology, Pima and Tohono O'odham ethnologies, archaeological theory, regional geology and geomorphology, botany, and zooarchaeology.

The purpose of this master file is to eliminate frequent typing and proofreading of commonly cited references. Entries in the master are correctly cited according to the guidelines presented in Chapter 3 and contain all necessary information.

Each entry in the master bibliography is identified by a file name (a combination of the author's name and the date of publication). Authors who use the Museum's computer equipment to produce manuscripts may use these files to create their reference lists. Also an author may compile a list of file names for the entries cited and the references may be assembled by a secretary or the editor.

To use the master obtain a printed copy of the bibliography (from the CRMD office), record the file name of each reference cited, and provide cards for cited references that are not included in the master. Sample entries are provided below. File names are in capital letters and precede each entry.

ADAMS. E. C/19781
Adams, E. Charles
1978 The Function of Limited Activity Sites in the Settlement System of the Lower Piedra District, Colorado. In "Limited Activity and Occupation Sites: A Collection of Conference Papers," compiled and edited by Albert E. Ward. *Contributions to Anthropological Studies* 1: 99–108. Albuquerque: Center for Anthropological Studies.

ADAMS. E. C/19811
Adams, E. Charles
1981 The View from the Hopi Mesas. In "The Protohistoric Period in the North American Southwest, A.D. 1450–1700," edited by David R. Wilcox and W. Bruce Masse. *Arizona State University Anthropological Research Papers* 42: 321–335. Tempe: Arizona State University.

ADAMS. E. D/19741
Adams, E. D.
1974 *Soil Survey: Eastern Maricopa and Northern Pinal Counties Area, Arizona*. Soil Conservation Service, in cooperation with Arizona Agricultural Experiment Station. Washington: U.S. Department of Agriculture.

REFERENCES AND RECOMMENDED SOURCES OF INFORMATION

American Geological Institute
1974 *Dictionary of Geological Terms*. Garden City: Doubleday.

American Ornithologists' Union
1957 *A.O.U. Check List of North American Birds*, 5th edition. Baltimore: Port City Press.

Barnes, Will C.
1988 *Arizona Place Names*. Tucson: University of Arizona Press.
Barnes is preferred to Granger's (1982) revised and enlarged version of *Arizona Place Names*, although Granger should be consulted for spelling of place names not found in Barnes.

Barzun, Jacques, and Henry F. Graff
1977 *The Modern Researcher*, 3d edition. New York: Harcourt Brace Jovanovich.

Benson, Lyman
1969 *The Cacti of Arizona*, 3d edition. Tucson: University of Arizona Press.

Benson, Lyman, and Robert A. Darrow
1981 *Trees and Shrubs of the Southwestern Deserts*, 3d edition. Tucson: University of Arizona Press.

Bernstein, Theodore M.
1978 *The Careful Writer*. New York: Atheneum.

Chisholm, L. J.
1967 Units of Weight and Measure. *National Bureau of Standards Miscellaneous Publication* 286. Washington: U.S. Department of Commerce.

Cockrum, Lendell E.
1960 *The Recent Mammals of Arizona*. Tucson: University of Arizona Press.

Committee on the Names of Fishes, R. M. Bailey, Chairman
1966 A List of Common and Scientific Names of Fishes from the United States and Canada. *Report of the Committee of the American Fisheries Society Special Publication* 2. Arlington: Cooper-Trent Lithograph.

Day, Robert A.
1983 *How to Write and Publish a Scientific Paper*, 2d edition. Philadelphia: ISI Press.

Diem, Konrad, editor
1962 *Scientific Tables*. Documenta Geigy, 6th Edition. Basle, Switzerland: CIBA-GEIGY Lmt.

Fowler, Henry W.
1965 *A Dictionary of Modern English Usage*, 2d edition, revised by Sir Ernest Gowers. Oxford: Clarendon Press.

Granger, Byrd H.
1982 *Arizona Place Names*, 2d edition. Tucson: University of Arizona Press.

Harrison, Margaret W.
1945 The Writing of American Archaeology. *American Antiquity* 10(4): 331–339.

Hoffmeister, Donald F.
1986 *Mammals of Arizona*. Tucson: University of Arizona Press.

Huckell, Bruce B.
1983 Additional Chronological Data on Cienega Valley, Arizona. In "Cultural and Environmental History of Cienega Valley, Southeastern Arizona," by Frank W. Eddy and Maurice E. Cooley. *Anthropological Papers of the University of Arizona* 43: 57–58. Tucson: University of Arizona Press.

Jones, J. Knox, Jr., Dilford C. Carter, Hugh H. Genoways, Robert S. Hoffmann, Dale W. Rice, and Clyde Jones
1986 Revised Checklist of North American Mammals North of Mexico, 1986. *Occasional Papers, The Museum, Texas Tech University* 107: 1–22. Lubbock: Texas Tech University Press.

Kearney, Thomas H., and Robert Peebles
1960 *Arizona Flora*. Berkeley and Los Angeles: University of California Press.

Keen, A. Myra
1971 *Sea Shells of Tropical West America*, 2d edition. Stanford: Stanford University Press.

Klein, Jeffrey, J. C. Lerman, Paul E. Damon, and E. K. Ralph
1982 Calibration of Radiocarbon Dates: Tables Based on the Consensus Data of the Workshop on Calibrating the Radiocarbon Time Scale. *Radiocarbon* 24(2): 103–150.

Lehr, J. Harry
1978 *A Catalogue of the Flora of Arizona*. Phoenix: Desert Botanial Garden. (Printed by Northland Press, Flagstaff, Arizona.)

Lowe, Charles H.
1964 *Arizona's Natural Environment*. Tucson: University of Arizona Press.
1976 *The Vertebrates of Arizona*. Tucson: University of Arizona Press.

Miller, Gerrit S., Jr., and Remington Kellogg
1955 List of North American Recent Mammals. *United States National Museum Bulletin* 205. Washington: Smithsonian Institution.

Nicholson, Margaret
1957 *A Dictionary of American-English Usage: Based on Fowler's Modern English Usage*. New York: Oxford University Press.

Rice, Prudence M.
1987 *Pottery Analysis, A Sourcebook*. Chicago: University of Chicago Press.

Schmidt, Karl P.
1953 *A Check List of North American Amphibians and Reptiles*, 6th edition. Chicago: University of Chicago Press.

Scroggins, Mary J.
1988 Editorial Consistency Enhances Readability. *The Editorial Eye* 11(11), November 1988: 1–2. Alexandria: Editorial Experts, Inc.

Shepard Anna O.
1956 Ceramics for the Archaeologist. *Carnegie Institution of Washington Publication* 573. Washington.

Strunk, William, Jr., and E. B. White
1972 *The Elements of Style*, 2d edition. New York: Macmillan.

University of Chicago Press
1982 *The Chicago Manual of Style*, 13th edition, revised and expanded. Chicago: University of Chicago Press.

Vogler, Lawrence E.
1980 The Arizona State Museum Archaeological Site Survey System. *Arizona State Museum Archaeological Series* 128. Tucson: Arizona State Museum, University of Arizona.

Webster's Seventh New Collegiate Dictionary
1969 Springfield, Massachusetts: Merriam.
(Any recent edition may be used.)

Webster's Third New International Dictionary of the English Language, Unabridged.
1961 Springfield, Massachusetts: Merriam.

Appendix A

SCIENTIFIC AND COMMON NAMES OF PLANT SPECIES FREQUENTLY RECOVERED IN THE SOUTHWEST

Scientific Name	Common Name
Pinaceae	pine family
Pinus	pine
P. cembroides	Mexican pinyon
P. edulis	pinyon pine
P. engelmannii	Arizona longleaf pine, Apache pine
P. ponderosa	ponderosa pine
Cupressaceae	cypress family
Cupressus	cypress
C. arizonica	Arizona cypress
Juniperus	juniper
J. californica	California juniper
J. monosperma	one-seed juniper
Ephedraceae	joint-fir family
Ephedra	Mormon tea, Mexican tea
E. trifurca	Mexican tea
E. torreyana	Mormon tea
Typhaceae	cattail family
Typha	cattail
T. angustifolia	narrow-leaved cattail
T. domingensis	southern cattail
T. latifolia	broad-leaved cattail
Sparganiaceae	bur reed family
Sparganium	bur reed
Gramineae	grass family
Aristida	three-awn
Arundo	giant reed, carrizo
Bouteloua	grama
Bromus	bromegrass
Hordeum	
H. pusillum	little barley
Panicum	
P. sonorum	
P. dichotomiflorum	
Phragmites	common reed
P. australis	
Puccinellia	alkali grass
Setaria	bristle grass
Sporobolus	drop seed grass, Sacaton grass
Tripsacum	gama grass
Cyperaceae	sedge family
Carex	sedge
Cyperus	flat sedge
Scirpus	bulrush, tule
Liliaceae	lily family
Agavaceae	agave family
Agave	agave, century plant, maguey
A. arizonica	
A. desertii	desert agave
A. parryi	Parry agave
A. parviflora	small-flowered agave
A. palmeri	Palmer agave, mescal, century plant
A. murpheyi	
Dasylirion	sotol
D. wheeleri	desert spoon, sotol, palmea
Nolina	bear grass
Yucca	yucca, soap weed, Spanish bayonet, datil
Y. arizonica	
Y. baccata	banana yucca
Y. brevifolia	Joshua tree
Y. elata	soapweed
Y. glauca	Great Plains yucca
Salicaceae	willow family
Populus	cottonwood, poplar, aspen
P. arizonica	Arizona cottonwood
P. fremontii	Fremont cottonwood
P. tremuloides	quaking aspen
Salix	willow
Juglandaceae	walnut family
Juglans	walnut
J. major	Arizona walnut

Scientific Name	Common Name
Betulaceae	birch family
Alnus	alder
A. oblongifolia	Arizona alder
A. tenuifolia	thin-leaf alder
Fagaceae	beech family
Quercus	oak
Q. arizonica	Arizona white oak
Q. emoryi	Emory oak
Q. gambelii	Gambel oak
Ulmaceae	elm family
Celtis	hackberry
C. pallida	desert hackberry
C. reticulata	net leaf hackberry
Polygonaceae	buckwheat family
Chorizanthe	
C. thurberi	Thurber spiny herb
C. watsoni	Watson spiny herb
Eriogonum	wild buckwheat
E. fasciculatum	
E. deserticola	
Polygonum	
Rumex	dock, sorrel
Chenopodiaceae	goose foot family
Allenrolfea	iodine bush
A. occidentalis	pickleweed
Atriplex	salt bush
A. acanthocarpa	
A. argentea	
A. canescens	four-wing salt bush
A. elegans	
A. lentiformis	quail brush, lens scale
A. polycarpa	desert salt bush, cattle spinach
Chenopodium	goose foot, pigweed
C. ambrosioides	
C. berlandieri	
Monolepis	patata
M. nuttalliana	poverty weed
Nitrophila	
N. occidentalis	alkali weed
Salsola	Russian thistle
Sarcobatus	grease wood
Suaeda	seepweed, sea blight
S. suffrutescens	
S. torreyana	
S. fruticosa	alkali seepweed
Amaranthaceae	amaranth family
Tidestromia	tidestromia
Nyctaginaceae	four o'clock family
Boerhaavia	spiderling
B. coulteri	
Aizoaceae	carpet weed family
Mollugo	carpet weed
M. verticillata	Indian chick weed

Scientific Name	Common Name
Trianthema	horse purslane
T. portulacastrum	
Portulacaceae	portulaca family
Calandrinia	rock purslane
Portulaca	purslane
Caryophyllaceae	pink family
Arenaria	sand wort
Silene	catchfly, campion
Cruciferae	mustard family
Descurainia	tansy mustard
Lepidium	pepper grass, pepperwort
Cleomaceae	cleome family
Cleome	spider flower, bee plant
C. serrulata	beeweed
Polanisia	clammy weed
Platanaceae	plane tree family
Platanus	sycamore
P. wrightii	Arizona sycamore
Leguminosae	pea family
Mimosoideae	mimosa or acacia subfamily
Acacia	acacia
A. constricta	white thorn
A. greggii	cat claw
Prosopis	mesquite
P. juliflora	
P. glandulosa	
P. pubescens	
P. velutina	
Caesalpinioideae	bird-of-paradise subfamily
Cercidium	
C. floridum	blue palo verde
C. microphyllum	foothill palo verde
Papilionoideae	bean subfamily
Astragalus	milk vetch, loco weed
Lupinus	lupine
Olneya	
O. tesota	ironwood
Phaseolus	bean
P. acutifolius	
P. acutifolius var. *latifolius*	tepary bean
P. lunatus	lima bean
P. multiflorus	scarlet runner bean
P. vulgaris	common bean
Canavalia	
C. ensiformis	jack bean
Geraniaceae	geranium family
Erodium	heron bill
Zygophyllaceae	caltrop family
Kallstroemia	
K. californica	
K. grandiflora	
K. parviflora	
Larrea	creosote bush
L. tridentata	creosote bush, greasewood

Scientific Name	Common Name
Euphorbiaceae	spurge family
Euphorbia	spurge
Anacardiaceae	cashew family, sumac family
Rhus trilobata	sumac, squaw bush
Malvaceae	mallow family
Gossypium	cotton
G. thurberi	desert cotton
G. hirsutum	native cotton
G. hopi	Hopi cotton
Malva	mallow, cheese weed
M. parviflora	little mallow
Sphaeralcea	alkali pink, globe mallow
Tamaricaceae	tamarix family
Tamarix	tamarisk
Loasaceae	stick leaf family
Mentzelia	stick leaf, blazing star
Cactaceae	cactus family
Cereus	
C. giganteus	saguaro cactus
C. greggii	night-blooming cereus
C. thurberi	organ pipe cactus
Echinocereus	hedgehog cactus
E. engelmannii	
E. fasciculatus	
E. fendleri	
E. pectinatus	rainbow cactus
Ferocactus	barrel cactus
Mammillaria	fishhook cactus, pincushion cactus
Opuntia	prickly pear, cholla
subgenus *Cylindropuntia*	cholla
O. echinocarpa	silver cholla
O. acanthocarpa	buckhorn cholla
O. spinosior	cane cholla
O. versicolor	staghorn cholla
O. fulgida	jumping cholla
subgenus *Opuntia*	prickly pear
O. polycantha	prickly pear
O. fragilis	little prickly pear
O. basilaris	beavertail cactus
Onagraceae	evening primrose family
Fouquieriaceae	ocotillo or candlewood family
Fouquieria splendens	ocotillo, coachwhip
Oleaceae	olive family
Fraxinus	ash
F. velutina	Arizona ash
Hydrophyllaceae	water leaf family
Phacelia	
Boraginaceae	borage family
Amsinckia	fiddle neck
Labiatae	mint family
Solanaceae	potato family, nightshade family
Capsicum	red pepper
Datura	jimson weed
Lycium	wolfberry, desert thorn
Nicotiana	tobacco
N. glauca	
N. rustica	
Physalis	*ground cherry*
P. acutifolia	
Solanum	nightshade
Plantaginaceae	plantain family
Plantago	plantain, Indian wheat
Cucurbitaceae	gourd family
Cucurbita	squashes and pumpkins
C. digitata	coyote melon
C. foetidissima	buffalo gourd
C. pepo	
C. moschata	moschata squash
C. mixta	cushaw
Lagenaria siceraria	cultivated gourd
Compositae	sunflower family
Ambrosia	ragweed, bur sage
A. deltoidea	bur sage
Artemisia	wormwood, sagebrush
Baccharis	
B. glutinosa	seep willow
B. sarathroides	desert broom
Berlandiera	green eyes
Chrysothamnus	rabbit brush
C. greenei	
C. nauseous	
Haplopappus	
H. tenuisectus	burro weed
H. pluriflorus	Jimmy weed
Helianthus	sunflower
Pluchea	marsh fleabane, stinkweed
Xanthocephalum	broomweed, snakeweed
Zinnia acerosa	desert zinnia

Races of maize recovered from archaeological sites in the Southwest:

- Chapalote
- Reventador
- Onaveño
- Mais Blando de Sonora
- 8-Rowed, or Harinoso de Ocho

Appendix B

SCIENTIFIC AND COMMON NAMES OF ANIMAL SPECIES FREQUENTLY RECOVERED IN THE SOUTHWEST

Scientific Name	Common Name
OSTEICHTHYES	bony fish
Cypriniformes	
Cyprinidae	
Ptychocheilus lucius	Colorado River squawfish
Catostomidae	
Catostomus latipinnis	flannelmouth sucker
Catostomus sp.	sucker
Pantosteus clarki	Gila Mountain sucker
Xyrauchen texanus	humpback sucker
Gila cypha	humpback chub
AMPHIBIA	amphibians
Pelobatidae	spadefoot toads
Scaphiopus couchi	Couch's spadefoot
Bufonidae	
Bufo alvarius	Colorado River toad
B. woodhousei	Woodhouse's toad
B. cognatus	Great Plains toad
Ranidae	
Rana pipiens	leopard frog
REPTILIA	reptiles
Kinosternidae	
Kinosternon sonoriense	Sonoran mud turtle
Emydidae	
Terrapene ornata	western box turtle
Testudinidae	
Gopherus agassizi	desert tortoise
Iguanidae	
Crotaphytus collaris	collared lizard
Sceloporus undulatus	eastern fence lizard
S. magister	desert spiny lizard
Phrynosoma solare	regal horned lizard
Uta stansburiana	side-blotched lizard
Teiidae	
Cnemidophorus velox	plateau whiptail
C. tigris	western whiptail
Crotalidae	pit vipers
Crotalus	rattlesnakes
C. atrox	western diamondback rattlesnake
C. scutulatus	Mohave rattlesnake
Colubridae	colubrid snakes
Thamnophis cf. *T. elegans*	Western garter snake
Masticophis flagellum	coachwhip
Elaphe cf. *E. triaspis*	green rat snake
Lampropeltis cf. *L. pyromelana*	Sonora mountain kingsnake
AVES	birds
Anatidae	
Branta canadensis	Canada goose
Anser albifrons	white-fronted goose
Chen caerulescens	snow goose
Anas platyrhynchos	mallard
A. acuta	pintail
A. strepera	gadwall
A. carolinensis	green-winged teal
Cathartidae	
Cathartes aura	turkey vulture
Accipitridae	
Accipiter gentilis	goshawk
A. striatus	sharp-shinned hawk
A. cooperi	Cooper's hawk
Buteo jamaicensis	red-tailed hawk
B. swainsoni	Swainson's hawk
B. lagopus	rough-legged hawk
B. regalis	ferruginous hawk
Aquila chrysaetos	golden eagle
Haliaeetus leucocephalus	bald eagle
Falconidae	
Falco mexicanus	prairie falcon
F. sparvarius	sparrow hawk

Scientific Name	Common Name
Phasianidae	
Lophortyx gambelii or *Callipepla gambelii*	Gambel's quail
C. squamata	scaled quail
Cyrtonyx montezumae	harlequin quail
Rallidae	
Fulica americana	American coot
Meleagrididae	
Meleagris gallopavo	turkey
Gruidae	
Grus canadensis	lesser sandhill crane
Columbidae	
Zenaidura (Zenaida) macroura	mourning dove
Psittacidae	
Rhynchopsitta pachyrhyncha	thick-billed parrot
Amazona albifrons	white-fronted parrot
Ara macao	scarlet macaw
Ara militaris	military macaw
Cuculidae	
Geococcyx californianus	roadrunner
Tytonidae	
Tyto alba	barn owl
Strigidae	
Otus asio	common screech owl
Bubo virginianus	great horned owl
Speotyto cunicularia	burrowing owl
Glaucidium gnoma	pygmy owl
Picidae	
Colaptes auratus	yellow-shafted flicker
Melanerpes formicivorus	acorn woodpecker
Centurus uropygialis	Gila woodpecker
Corvidae	
Cyanocitta stelleri	Steller's jay
Aphelocoma coerulescens	scrub jay
Pica pica	black-billed magpie
Corvus corax	common raven
C. brachrhynchos	common crow
C. cryptoleucus	white-necked raven
Gymnorhinus cyanocephalus	pinyon jay
Troglodytidae	
Troglodytes aedon	house wren
Mimidae	
Mimus polyglottos	mockingbird
Toxostoma	thrashers
Oreoscoptes montanus	sage thrasher
Turdidae	
Sialia mexicana	western bluebird
Icteridae	
Xanthocephalus xanthocephalus	yellow-headed blackbird

Scientific Name	Common Name
Agelaius phoeniceus	red-winged blackbird
Euphagus cycanocephalus	Brewer's blackbird
MAMMALIA	Mammals
Insectivora	Insectivores
Soricidae	shrews
Sorex arizonae	Arizona shrew
S. merriami	Merriam's shrew
S. monticolus	dusky or montane shrew
S. nanus	dwarf shrew
S. palustris	water shrew
Notiosorex crawfordi	desert shrew
Chiroptera	Bats
Mormoopidae	ghost-faced bats and relatives
Mormoops megalophylla	ghost-faced bat
Phyllostomidae	American leaf-nosed bats
Macrotus californicus	California leaf-nosed bat
Choeronycteris mexicana	Mexican long-tongued bat
Leptonycteris sanborni	Sanborn's long-nosed bat
Vespertilionidae	Vespertilionid bats
Myotis yumanensis	Yuma myotis
M. velifer	cave myotis
M. occultus	Arizona myotis
M. evotis	long-eared myotis
M. auriculus	Southwestern myotis
M. thysanodes	fringed myotis
M. volans	long-legged myotis
M. californicus	California myotis
M. leibii	small-footed myotis
Lasionycteris noctivagans	silver-haired bat
Pipistrellus hesperus	Western pipistrelle
Eptesicus fuscus	big brown bat
Lasiurus borealis	red bat
L. ega	Southern yellow bat
L. cinereus	hoary bat
Euderma maculatum	spotted bat
Idionycteris phyllotis	Allen's lappet-browned or big-eared bat
Plecotus townsendii	Townsend's big-eared bat
Antrozous pallidus	pallid bat
Molossidae	free-tailed bats
Tadarida brasiliensis	Brazilian or American free-tailed bat
T. femorosacca	pocketed free-tailed bat
T. macrotis	big free-tailed bat
Eumops perotis	Western mastiff bat
E. underwoodi	Underwood's mastiff bat
Lagomorpha	Lagomorphs
Leporidae	rabbits and hares
Sylvilagus floridanus	eastern cottontail
S. nuttallii	Nuttall's or mountain cottontail

Scientific Name	Common Name
S. audubonii	desert cottontail
Lepus californicus	black-tailed jackrabbit
L. alleni	antelope jackrabbit
Rodentia	Rodents
Sciuridae	squirrels
Eutamias (= Tamias) minimus	least chipmunk
E. (= T.) quadrivittatus	Colorado chipmunk
E. (= T.) dorsalis	cliff chipmunk
E. (= T.) umbrinus	Uinta chipmunk
E. (= T.) cinereicollis	gray-collared chipmunk
Ammospermophilus leucurus	white-tailed antelope squirrel
A. harrisii	Harris' antelope squirrel
Spermophilus tridecemlineatus	thirteen-lined ground squirrel
S. variegatus	rock squirrel
S. spilosoma	spotted ground squirrel
S. tereticaudus	round-tailed ground squirrel
S. lateralis	golden-mantled ground squirrel
Cynomys ludovicianus	black-tailed prairie dog
C. gunnisoni	Gunnison's prairie dog
Sciurus aberti	Abert's squirrel
S. arizonensis	Arizona gray squirrel
S. nayaritensis	Mexican fox squirrel or Nayarit squirrel
Tamiasciurus hudsonicus	red squirrel
Geomyidae	pocket gophers
Thomomys bottae	Botta's pocket gopher
T. umbrinus	Southern pocket gopher
T. talpoides	Northern pocket gopher
Heteromyidae	kangaroo rats, pocket mice
Perognathus longimembris	little pocket mouse
P. amplus	Arizona pocket mouse
P. apache	Apache pocket mouse
P. flavus	silky pocket mouse
P. parvus	Great Basin pocket mouse
P. formosus	long-tailed pocket mouse
Perognathus (= Chaetodipus) intermedius	rock pocket mouse
P. (= C.) penicillatus	desert pocket mouse
P. (= C.) baileyi	Bailey's pocket mouse
P. (= C.) hispidus	hispid pocket mouse
Dipodomys ordii	Ord's kangaroo rat
D. microps	chisel-toothed kangaroo rat
D. spectabilis	banner-tailed kangaroo rat
D. merriami	Merriam's kangaroo rat

Scientific Name	Common Name
D. deserti	desert kangaroo rat
Castoridae	beavers
Castor canadensis	beaver
Cricetidae	New World mice and rats
Reithrodontomys montanus	Plains harvest mouse
R. megalotis	Western harvest mouse
R. fulvescens	fulvous harvest mouse
Peromyscus eremicus	cactus mouse
P. merriami	Merriam's or mesquite mouse
P. crinitus	canyon mouse
P. maniculatus	deer mouse
P. leucopus	white-footed mouse
P. boylii	brush mouse
P. truei	pinyon mouse
P. difficilis	rock mouse
Baiomys taylori	Northern pygmy mouse
Onychomys leucogaster	Northern grasshopper mouse
O. torridus	Southern grasshopper mouse
Sigmodon hispidus	hispid cotton rat
S. arizonae	Arizona cotton rat
S. fulviventer	fulvous or tawny-bellied cotton rat
S. ochrognathus	yellow-nosed cotton rat
Neotoma albigula	white-throated wood rat
N. lepida	desert wood rat
N. stephensi	Stephen's wood rat
N. mexicana	Mexican wood rat
N. cinerea	bushy-tailed wood rat
Microtinae	voles and lemmings
Clethrionomys gapperi	Southern red-backed mouse or vole
Microtus montanus	montane vole
M. longicaudus	long-tailed vole
M. mexicanus	Mexican vole
Ondatra zibethicus	muskrat
Zapodidae	jumping mice
Zapus hudsonius	meadow jumping mouse
Z. princeps	western jumping mouse
Erethizontidae	New World porcupines
Erethizon dorsatum	porcupine
Carnivora	carnivores
Canidae	canids
Canis familiaris	domestic dog
C. latrans	coyote
C. lupus	gray wolf
Vulpes vulpes	red fox
V. macrotis	kit fox

Scientific Name	Common Name
MAMMALIA, Carnivora (continued)	
V. velox	swift fox
Urocyon cinereoargenteus	gray fox
Ursidae	bears
Ursus arctos (= *horribilis)*	grizzly or brown bear
U. americanus	black bear
Procyonidae	raccoons and relatives
Procyon lotor	raccoon
Nasua nasua	coati
Bassariscus astutus	ringtail
Mustelidae	weasels, skunks, and relatives
Mustela frenata	long-tailed weasel
M. nigripes	black-footed ferret
Taxidea taxus	badger
Spilogale gracilis	Western spotted skunk
Mephitis mephitis	striped skunk
M. macroura	hooded skunk
Conepatus mesoleucus	hog-nosed skunk
Lutra canadensis	river otter
Felidae	cats
Felis onca	jaguar
F. pardalis	ocelot
F. concolor	mountain lion
F. (= Lynx) rufus	bobcat
Artiodactyla	even-toed ungulates
Tayassuidae	peccaries and pigs
Tayassu tajacu	collared peccary
Cervidae	deer, wapiti (elk), and relatives
Cervis elaphus	wapiti or American elk
Odocoileus hemionus	mule or black-tailed deer
O. virginianus	white-tailed deer
Antilocapridae	pronghorns
Antilocapra americana	pronghorn
Bovidae	cattle, sheep, and relatives
Ovis canadensis	bighorn or mountain sheep
Bos taurus	domestic cattle
Bison bison	bison

Appendix C

SCIENTIFIC NAMES OF SHELL SPECIES FREQUENTLY RECOVERED IN THE SOUTHWEST

Spellings and genus and subgenus classifications follow Keen (1971). Classifications used by other authors are given in parentheses where appropriate, but preferred style is to follow Keen.

Marine Shells

Acanthina,
see *Neorapana tuberculata*
Acmaea sp.
Aequipecten,
see *Argopecten circularis*
Agaronia hiatula
Agaronia propatula
(= *A. testacca*)
Anachis coronata
Anomalocardia,
see *Chione subimbricata*
Arca sp.
Arca pacifica
Argopecten circularis
(= *Aequipecten*)
Avicula peruviana
(= *Pteria*)
Cadulus sp.
Cantharus,
see *Solenosteira macrospira*
Cardium,
see *Trachycardium panamense*
Cerithidea albonodosa
Cerithidea californica
Cerithidea mazatlanica
Cerithidea montagnei
Cerithium menkei
Cerithium stercusmuscarum
Chama buddiana
Chama echinata
Chione californiensis
Chione fluctifraga
Chione gnidia
Chione subimbricata
(= *Anomalocardia*)
Chione undatella
Codakia distinguenda
Codakia fuscata
Collisella stanfordiana
(= *Nomaeopelta*)
Columbella aureomexicana
Columbella major
Columbella strombiformis
(= *Pyrene*)
Conus californicus
Conus gladiator
Conus perplexus
Conus princeps
Conus purpurascens
Conus regularis
Conus ximenes
Corbula nasuta
Crepidula onyx
Crepidula striolata
Crucibulum spinosum
Cypraea annettae
Dentalium neohexagonum
Dentalium oerstedii
Dentalium semipolitum
Diodora inaequalis
Donax gouldii
Donax gracilis
Dosinia ponderosa
Erato sp.
Fasciolaria sp.
Galiodea,
see *Melongena patula*
Glycymeris gigantea
Glycymeris maculata
Glycymeris multicostata
(= *G. bicolor*)
Glycymeris strigilata
(= *G. tessellata*)
Haliotis assimilis
Haliotis cracherodii
Haliotis corrugata
Haliotis fulgens
Haliotis rufescens
Laevicardium elatum
Lamellaria diegoensis
Lucina prolongata
Lyropecten subnodus
(= *Pecten*)
Malea ringens
Melongena patula
(= *Galiodea*)
Morula lugubris
Muricanthus nigritus
Nassa (Nassarius) leucops
Nassa tegula
Nassarius sp.
(= *Alectrion*)
Nassarius complanatus
Nassarius iodes
Nassarius moestus
Nassarius versicolor
Natica chemnitzii
Neorapana tuberculata
(= *Acanthina*)
Nerita funiculata
(= *N. bernhardi*)
Nerita scabricosta
Neritina sp.
Neritina picta,
see *Theodoxus luteofasciatus*
Nomaeopelta,
see *Collisella stanfordiana*
Oliva incrassata
(= *O. angulata*)
Oliva spicata
Oliva undatella
Olivella dama

Olivella fletcherae
Olivella gracilis
Olivella tergina
Olivella volutella
Olivella zanoeta
Ocenebra sp.
(= *Tritonalia* sp.)
Opalia sp.
Ostrea angelica
Ostrea fisheri
Panopea sp.
Pecten,
see *Lyropecten subnodus*
Pecten sp.
Pecten vogdesi
(= *P. excavatus*)
Persicula bandera
Phyllonotus sp.
Pinctada mazatlanica
Polinices sp.
Polinices recluzianus
Polinices uber
Pteria,
see *Avicula peruviana*
Pteria sterna
Pyrene,
see *Columbella* spp.
Serpulorbis sp.
(= *Aletes*)
Serpulorbis oryzata
Solenosteira macrospira
(= *Cantharus*)
Spondylus calcifer
(= *S. limbatus*)
Spondylus princeps
Strombus galeatus
Strombus gracilior
Strombus pugilis
Tagelus californianus
Tegula rugosa
Theodoxus luteofasciatus
(= *Neritina picta*)
Tivela sp.
Trachycardium panamense
(= *Cardium procerum*)
Trigoniocardia biangulata
Trigoniocardia granifera
Tripsycha tripsycha
Tritonalia,
see *Ocenebra*
Trivia radians
Trivia solandri
Turbo fluctuosus
Turritella gonostoma
Turritella leucostoma
(= *T. tigrina*)
Vermetus sp.
Vermicularia sp.

Freshwater Shells

Amnicola longingua
Anodonta californiensis
Gyraulus sp.
Helisoma tenue sinuosum
Helisoma cf. *trivolvis*
Lymnaea (Fossaria) dalli
Physa virgata
Pisidium sp.

Land Shells

Catinella avara
Gastrocopta cristata
Oreohelix houghi
Pupoides hordaceus
Rabdotus schiedeanus
Succinea sp.
Succinea avara

Appendix D

METRIC AND TEMPERATURE CONVERSIONS

Table D.1: Inches to centimeters and centimeters to inches
Table D.2: Feet to meters
Table D.3: Meters to feet
Table D.4: Miles to kilometers
Table D.5: Kilometers to miles
Table D.6: Fahrenheit to Centigrade and Centigrade to Fahrenheit

Conversion Tables D.1 and D.6 are reprinted from *Scientific Tables*, Documenta Geigy, 6th edition, edited by Konrad Diem, with permission of CIBA-GEIGY Limited, Basle, Switzerland, 1962. Conversion Tables D.2 through D.5 were compiled from Units of Weight and Measure (Chisholm 1967; *National Bureau of Standards Miscellaneous Publication* 286).

Conversion Formulas

To convert from	*to*	*multiply by*
Inches	millimeters	25.40
Inches	centimeters	2.54
Inches	meters	0.025
Feet	centimeters	30.48
Feet	meters	0.305
Miles	kilometers	1.609
Square miles	square kilometers	2.59
Acres	hectares	0.405
Millimeters	inches	0.039
Centimeters	inches	0.394
Centimeters	feet	0.033
Cubic centimeters	cubic inches	0.061
Meters	inches	39.37
Meters	feet	3.28
Meters	yards	1.093
Kilometers	miles	0.62
Hectares	acres	2.47
Ounces (Avoirdupois)	grams	28.35
Pounds (Avoirdupois)	grams	453.59
Grams	ounces (Avoirdupois)	0.035
Grams	pounds (Avoirdupois)	0.002

TABLE D.1. Conversion of Inches to Centimeters and Centimeters to Inches

Examples: (*a*) 45 in = 3 ft 9 in
(*b*) 60⅜ in = 153.4 cm; 2.23 in = 2 in + 0.23 in = 5.08 cm + 0.5842 cm = 5.6642 cm; 3 ft 8¾ in = 113.7 cm
(*c*) 101 cm = 39.764 in ≈ 3 ft 3¾ in; 10.1 cm = 3.9764 in

Inches or Feet and Inches – Centimeters

in	ft + in	0	⅛ (0.125)	¼ (0.25)	⅜ (0.375)	½ (0.5)	⅝ (0.625)	¾ (0.75)	⅞ (0.875)	in	ft + in	0	⅛ (0.125)	¼ (0.25)	⅜ (0.375)	½ (0.5)	⅝ (0.625)	¾ (0.75)	⅞ (0.875)
0	**0** 0	0.000	0.318	0.635	0.953	1.270	1.588	1.905	2.223	**54**	**4** 6	137.2	137.5	137.8	138.1	138.4	138.7	139.1	139.4
1	**0** 1	2.540	2.858	3.175	3.493	3.810	4.128	4.445	4.763	55	**4** 7	139.7	140.0	140.3	140.7	141.0	141.3	141.6	141.9
2	**0** 2	5.080	5.398	5.715	6.033	6.350	6.668	6.985	7.303	56	**4** 8	142.2	142.6	142.9	143.2	143.5	143.8	144.1	144.5
3	**0** 3	7.620	7.938	8.255	8.573	8.890	9.208	9.525	9.843	57	**4** 9	144.8	145.1	145.4	145.7	146.1	146.4	146.7	147.0
4	**0** 4	10.16	10.48	10.80	11.11	11.43	11.75	12.07	12.38	58	**4** 10	147.3	147.6	148.0	148.3	148.6	148.9	149.2	149.5
5	**0** 5	12.70	13.02	13.34	13.65	13.97	14.29	14.61	14.92	59	**4** 11	149.9	150.2	150.5	150.8	151.1	151.4	151.8	152.1
6	**0** 6	15.24	15.56	15.88	16.19	16.51	16.83	17.15	17.46	**60**	**5** 0	152.4	152.7	153.0	153.4	153.7	154.0	154.3	154.6
7	**0** 7	17.78	18.10	18.42	18.73	19.05	19.37	19.69	20.00	61	**5** 1	154.9	155.3	155.6	155.9	156.2	156.5	156.8	157.2
8	**0** 8	20.32	20.64	20.96	21.27	21.59	21.91	22.23	22.54	62	**5** 2	157.5	157.8	158.1	158.4	158.8	159.1	159.4	159.7
9	**0** 9	22.86	23.18	23.50	23.81	24.13	24.45	24.77	25.08	63	**5** 3	160.0	160.3	160.7	161.0	161.3	161.6	161.9	162.2
10	**0** 10	25.40	25.72	26.04	26.35	26.67	26.99	27.31	27.62	64	**5** 4	162.6	162.9	163.2	163.5	163.8	164.1	164.5	164.8
11	**0** 11	27.94	28.26	28.58	28.89	29.21	29.53	29.85	30.16	65	**5** 5	165.1	165.4	165.7	166.1	166.4	166.7	167.0	167.3
12	**1** 0	30.48	30.80	31.12	31.43	31.75	32.07	32.39	32.70	**66**	**5** 6	167.6	168.0	168.3	168.6	168.9	169.2	169.5	169.9
13	**1** 1	33.02	33.34	33.66	33.97	34.29	34.61	34.93	35.24	67	**5** 7	170.2	170.5	170.8	171.1	171.5	171.8	172.1	172.4
14	**1** 2	35.56	35.88	36.20	36.51	36.83	37.15	37.47	37.78	68	**5** 8	172.7	173.0	173.4	173.7	174.0	174.3	174.6	174.9
15	**1** 3	38.10	38.42	38.74	39.05	39.37	39.69	40.01	40.32	69	**5** 9	175.3	175.6	175.9	176.2	176.5	176.8	177.2	177.5
16	**1** 4	40.64	40.96	41.28	41.59	41.91	42.23	42.55	42.86	70	**5** 10	177.8	178.1	178.4	178.8	179.1	179.4	179.7	180.0
17	**1** 5	43.18	43.50	43.82	44.13	44.45	44.77	45.09	45.40	71	**5** 11	180.3	180.7	181.0	181.3	181.6	181.9	182.2	182.6
18	**1** 6	45.72	46.04	46.36	46.67	46.99	47.31	47.63	47.94	**72**	**6** 0	182.9	183.2	183.5	183.8	184.2	184.5	184.8	185.1
19	**1** 7	48.26	48.58	48.90	49.21	49.53	49.85	50.17	50.48	73	**6** 1	185.4	185.7	186.1	186.4	186.7	187.0	187.3	187.6
20	**1** 8	50.80	51.12	51.44	51.75	52.07	52.39	52.71	53.02	74	**6** 2	188.0	188.3	188.6	188.9	189.2	189.5	189.9	190.2
21	**1** 9	53.34	53.66	53.98	54.29	54.61	54.93	55.25	55.56	75	**6** 3	190.5	190.8	191.1	191.5	191.8	192.1	192.4	192.7
22	**1** 10	55.88	56.20	56.52	56.83	57.15	57.47	57.79	58.10	76	**6** 4	193.0	193.4	193.7	194.0	194.3	194.6	194.9	195.3
23	**1** 11	58.42	58.74	59.06	59.37	59.69	60.01	60.33	60.64	77	**6** 5	195.6	195.9	196.2	196.5	196.9	197.2	197.5	197.8
24	**2** 0	60.96	61.28	61.60	61.91	62.23	62.55	62.87	63.18	**78**	**6** 6	198.1	198.4	198.8	199.1	199.4	199.7	200.0	200.3
25	**2** 1	63.50	63.82	64.14	64.45	64.77	65.09	65.41	65.72	79	**6** 7	200.7	201.0	201.3	201.6	201.9	202.2	202.6	202.9
26	**2** 2	66.04	66.36	66.68	66.99	67.31	67.63	67.95	68.26	80	**6** 8	203.2	203.5	203.8	204.2	204.5	204.8	205.1	205.4
27	**2** 3	68.58	68.90	69.22	69.53	69.85	70.17	70.49	70.80	81	**6** 9	205.7	206.1	206.4	206.7	207.0	207.3	207.6	208.0
28	**2** 4	71.12	71.44	71.76	72.07	72.39	72.71	73.03	73.34	82	**6** 10	208.3	208.6	208.9	209.2	209.6	209.9	210.2	210.5
29	**2** 5	73.66	73.98	74.30	74.61	74.93	75.25	75.57	75.88	83	**6** 11	210.8	211.1	211.5	211.8	212.1	212.4	212.7	213.0
30	**2** 6	76.20	76.52	76.84	77.15	77.47	77.79	78.11	78.42	**84**	**7** 0	213.4	213.7	214.0	214.3	214.6	214.9	215.3	215.6
31	**2** 7	78.74	79.06	79.38	79.69	80.01	80.33	80.65	80.96	85	**7** 1	215.9	216.2	216.5	216.9	217.2	217.5	217.8	218.1
32	**2** 8	81.28	81.60	81.92	82.23	82.55	82.87	83.19	83.50	86	**7** 2	218.4	218.8	219.1	219.4	219.7	220.0	220.3	220.7
33	**2** 9	83.82	84.14	84.46	84.77	85.09	85.41	85.73	86.04	87	**7** 3	221.0	221.3	221.6	221.9	222.3	222.6	222.9	223.2
34	**2** 10	86.36	86.68	87.00	87.31	87.63	87.95	88.27	88.58	88	**7** 4	223.5	223.8	224.2	224.5	224.8	225.1	225.4	225.7
35	**2** 11	88.90	89.22	89.54	89.85	90.17	90.49	90.81	91.12	89	**7** 5	226.1	226.4	226.7	227.0	227.3	227.6	228.0	228.3
36	**3** 0	91.44	91.76	92.08	92.39	92.71	93.03	93.35	93.66	**90**	**7** 6	228.6	228.9	229.2	229.6	229.9	230.2	230.5	230.8
37	**3** 1	93.98	94.30	94.62	94.93	95.25	95.57	95.89	96.20	91	**7** 7	231.1	231.5	231.8	232.1	232.4	232.7	233.0	233.4
38	**3** 2	96.52	96.84	97.16	97.47	97.79	98.11	98.43	98.74	92	**7** 8	233.7	234.0	234.3	234.6	235.0	235.3	235.6	235.9
39	**3** 3	99.06	99.38	99.70	100.0	100.3	100.6	101.0	101.3	93	**7** 9	236.2	236.5	236.9	237.2	237.5	237.8	238.1	238.4
40	**3** 4	101.6	101.9	102.2	102.6	102.9	103.2	103.5	103.8	94	**7** 10	238.8	239.1	239.4	239.7	240.0	240.3	240.7	241.0
41	**3** 5	104.1	104.5	104.8	105.1	105.4	105.7	106.0	106.4	95	**7** 11	241.3	241.6	241.9	242.3	242.6	242.9	243.2	243.5
42	**3** 6	106.7	107.0	107.3	107.6	108.0	108.3	108.6	108.9	**96**	**8** 0	243.8	244.2	244.5	244.8	245.1	245.4	245.7	246.1
43	**3** 7	109.2	109.5	109.9	110.2	110.5	110.8	111.1	111.4	97	**8** 1	246.4	246.7	247.0	247.3	247.7	248.0	248.3	248.6
44	**3** 8	111.8	112.1	112.4	112.7	113.0	113.3	113.7	114.0	98	**8** 2	248.9	249.2	249.6	249.9	250.2	250.5	250.8	251.1
45	**3** 9	114.3	114.6	114.9	115.3	115.6	115.9	116.2	116.5	99	**8** 3	251.5	251.8	252.1	252.4	252.7	253.0	253.4	253.7
46	**3** 10	116.8	117.2	117.4	117.8	118.1	118.4	118.7	119.1	100	**8** 4	254.0	254.3	254.6	255.0	255.3	255.6	255.9	256.2
47	**3** 11	119.4	119.7	120.0	120.3	120.7	121.0	121.3	121.6	101	**8** 5	256.5	256.9	257.2	257.5	257.8	258.1	258.4	258.8
48	**4** 0	121.9	122.2	122.6	122.9	123.2	123.5	123.8	124.1	**102**	**8** 6	259.1	259.4	259.7	260.0	260.4	260.7	261.0	261.3
49	**4** 1	124.5	124.8	125.1	125.4	125.7	126.0	126.4	126.7	103	**8** 7	261.6	261.9	262.3	262.6	262.9	263.2	263.5	263.8
50	**4** 2	127.0	127.3	127.6	128.0	128.3	128.6	128.9	129.2	104	**8** 8	264.2	264.5	264.8	265.1	265.4	265.7	266.1	266.4
51	**4** 3	129.5	129.9	130.2	130.5	130.8	131.1	131.4	131.8	105	**8** 9	266.7	267.0	267.3	267.7	268.0	268.3	268.6	268.9
52	**4** 4	132.1	132.4	132.7	133.0	133.4	133.7	134.0	134.3	106	**8** 10	269.2	269.6	269.9	270.2	270.5	270.8	271.1	271.5
53	**4** 5	134.6	134.9	135.3	135.6	135.9	136.2	136.5	136.8	107	**8** 11	271.8	272.1	272.4	272.7	273.1	273.4	273.7	274.0

Centimeters – Inches or Feet and Inches

cm	0		1		2		3		4		5		6		7		8		9	
	in	ft+in†	in	ft+in†	in	ft+in†	in	ft+in†	in	ft+in†	in	ft+in†	in	ft+in†	in	ft+in†	in	ft+in†	in	ft+in†
0	0.0000	0 0	0.3937	0 0⅜	0.7874	0 0¾	1.1811	0 1⅛	1.5748	0 1⅝	1.9685	0 2	2.3622	0 2⅜	2.7559	0 2¾	3.1496	0 3⅛	3.5433	0 3½
10	3.9370	0 3⅞	4.3307	0 4⅜	4.7244	0 4¾	5.1181	0 5⅛	5.5118	0 5½	5.9055	0 5⅞	6.2992	0 6¼	6.6929	0 6¾	7.0866	0 7⅛	7.4803	0 7½
20	7.8740	0 7⅞	8.2677	0 8¼	8.6614	0 8⅝	9.0551	0 9	9.4488	0 9½	9.8425	0 9⅞	10.236	0 10¼	10.630	0 10⅝	11.024	0 11	11.417	0 11⅜
30	11.811	0 11¾	12.205	1 0¼	12.598	1 0⅝	12.992	1 1	13.386	1 1⅜	13.780	1 1¾	14.173	1 2⅛	14.567	1 2⅝	14.961	1 3	15.354	1 3⅜
40	15.748	1 3¾	16.142	1 4⅛	16.535	1 4½	16.929	1 4⅞	17.323	1 5⅜	17.717	1 5¾	18.110	1 6⅛	18.504	1 6½	18.898	1 6⅞	19.291	1 7¼
50	19.685	1 7⅝	20.079	1 8⅛	20.472	1 8½	20.866	1 8⅞	21.260	1 9¼	21.654	1 9⅝	22.047	1 10	22.441	1 10½	22.835	1 10⅞	23.228	1 11¼
60	23.622	1 11⅝	24.016	2 0	24.409	2 0⅜	24.803	2 0¾	25.197	2 1¼	25.591	2 1⅝	25.984	2 2	26.378	2 2⅜	26.772	2 2¾	27.165	2 3⅛
70	27.559	2 3½	27.953	2 4	28.346	2 4⅜	28.740	2 4¾	29.134	2 5⅛	29.528	2 5½	29.921	2 5⅞	30.315	2 6⅜	30.709	2 6¾	31.102	2 7⅛
80	31.496	2 7½	31.890	2 7⅞	32.283	2 8¼	32.677	2 8⅝	33.071	2 9⅛	33.465	2 9½	33.858	2 9⅞	34.252	2 10¼	34.646	2 10⅝	35.039	2 11
90	35.433	2 11⅜	35.827	2 11⅞	36.220	3 0¼	36.614	3 0⅝	37.008	3 1	37.402	3 1⅜	37.795	3 1¾	38.189	3 2¼	38.583	3 2⅝	38.976	3 3
100	39.370	3 3⅜	39.764	3 3¾	40.157	3 4⅛	40.551	3 4½	40.945	3 5	41.339	3 5⅜	41.732	3 5¾	42.126	3 6⅛	42.520	3 6½	42.913	3 6⅞
110	43.307	3 7¼	43.701	3 7¾	44.094	3 8⅛	44.488	3 8½	44.882	3 8⅞	45.276	3 9¼	45.669	3 9⅝	46.063	3 10⅛	46.457	3 10½	46.850	3 10⅞
120	47.244	3 11¼	47.638	3 11⅝	48.031	4 0	48.425	4 0⅜	48.819	4 0⅞	49.213	4 1¼	49.606	4 1⅝	50.000	4 2	50.394	4 2⅜	50.787	4 2¾
130	51.181	4 3⅛	51.575	4 3⅝	51.968	4 4	52.362	4 4⅜	52.756	4 4¾	53.150	4 5⅛	53.543	4 5½	53.937	4 5⅞	54.331	4 6⅜	54.724	4 6¾
140	55.118	4 7⅛	55.512	4 7½	55.905	4 7⅞	56.299	4 8¼	56.693	4 8¾	57.087	4 9⅛	57.480	4 9½	57.874	4 9⅞	58.268	4 10¼	58.661	4 10⅝
150	59.055	4 11	59.449	4 11½	59.842	4 11⅞	60.236	5 0¼	60.630	5 0⅝	61.024	5 1	61.417	5 1⅜	61.811	5 1¾	62.205	5 2¼	62.598	5 2⅝
160	62.992	5 3	63.386	5 3⅜	63.779	5 3¾	64.173	5 4⅛	64.567	5 4⅝	64.961	5 5	65.354	5 5⅜	65.748	5 5¾	66.142	5 6⅛	66.535	5 6½
170	66.929	5 6⅞	67.323	5 7⅜	67.716	5 7¾	68.110	5 8⅛	68.504	5 8½	68.898	5 8⅞	69.291	5 9¼	69.685	5 9⅝	70.079	5 10⅛	70.472	5 10½
180	70.866	5 10⅞	71.260	5 11¼	71.653	5 11⅝	72.047	6 0	72.441	6 0½	72.835	6 0⅞	73.228	6 1¼	73.622	6 1⅝	74.016	6 2	74.409	6 2⅜
190	74.803	6 2¾	75.197	6 3¼	75.590	6 3⅝	75.984	6 4	76.378	6 4⅜	76.772	6 4¾	77.165	6 5⅛	77.559	6 5½	77.953	6 6	78.346	6 6⅜
200	78.740	6 6¾	79.134	6 7⅛	79.527	6 7½	79.921	6 7⅞	80.315	6 8⅜	80.709	6 8¾	81.102	6 9⅛	81.496	6 9½	81.890	6 9⅞	82.283	6 10¼
210	82.677	6 10⅝	83.071	6 11⅛	83.464	6 11½	83.858	6 11⅞	84.252	7 0¼	84.646	7 0⅝	85.039	7 1	85.433	7 1⅜	85.827	7 1⅞	86.220	7 2¼
220	86.614	7 2⅝	87.008	7 3	87.401	7 3⅜	87.795	7 3¾	88.189	7 4¼	88.583	7 4⅝	88.976	7 5	89.370	7 5⅜	89.764	7 5¾	90.157	7 6⅛
230	90.551	7 6½	90.945	7 7	91.338	7 7⅜	91.732	7 7¾	92.126	7 8⅛	92.520	7 8½	92.913	7 8⅞	93.307	7 9¼	93.701	7 9¾	94.094	7 10⅛
240	94.488	7 10½	94.882	7 10⅞	95.275	7 11¼	95.669	7 11⅝	96.063	8 0⅛	96.457	8 0½	96.850	8 0⅞	97.244	8 1¼	97.638	8 1⅝	98.031	8 2
250	98.425	8 2⅜	98.819	8 2⅞	99.212	8 3¼	99.606	8 3⅝	100.00	8 4	100.39	8 4⅜	100.79	8 4¾	101.18	8 5⅛	101.57	8 5⅝	101.97	8 6
260	102.36	8 6⅜	102.76	8 6¾	103.15	8 7⅛	103.54	8 7½	103.94	8 8	104.33	8 8⅜	104.72	8 8¾	105.12	8 9⅛	105.51	8 9½	105.91	8 9⅞
270	106.30	8 10¼	106.69	8 10¾	107.09	8 11⅛	107.48	8 11½	107.87	8 11⅞	108.27	9 0¼	108.66	9 0⅝	109.05	9 1	109.45	9 1½	109.84	9 1⅞
280	110.24	9 2¼	110.63	9 2⅝	111.02	9 3	111.42	9 3⅜	111.81	9 3¾	112.20	9 4¼	112.60	9 4⅝	112.99	9 5	113.39	9 5⅜	113.78	9 5¾
290	114.17	9 6⅛	114.57	9 6⅝	114.96	9 7	115.35	9 7⅜	115.75	9 7¾	116.14	9 8⅛	116.54	9 8½	116.93	9 8⅞	117.32	9 9⅜	117.72	9 9¾

* Reproduction only by permission of the publishers of these *Scientific Tables*. † Rounded off to the nearest one-eighth inch.

TABLE D.2. Conversion of Feet to Meters

Examples: 96 feet = 29.26 meters   1 foot = 0.3048 meter
450 feet = 137.16 meters

Feet	0	1	2	3	4	5	6	7	8	9
	m	m	m	m	m	m	m	m	m	m
0	0.00	0.31	0.61	0.91	1.22	1.52	1.83	2.13	2.44	2.74
10	3.05	3.35	3.66	3.96	4.27	4.57	4.88	5.18	5.49	5.79
20	6.10	6.40	6.71	7.01	7.32	7.62	7.93	8.23	8.53	8.84
30	9.14	9.45	9.75	10.06	10.36	10.67	10.97	11.28	11.58	11.89
40	12.19	12.50	12.80	13.11	13.41	13.72	14.02	14.33	14.63	14.94
50	15.24	15.55	15.85	16.15	16.46	16.76	17.07	17.37	17.68	17.98
60	18.29	18.59	18.90	19.20	19.51	19.81	20.12	20.42	20.73	21.03
70	21.34	21.64	21.95	22.25	22.56	22.86	23.17	23.47	23.77	24.08
80	24.38	24.69	24.99	25.30	25.60	25.91	26.21	26.52	26.82	27.13
90	27.43	27.74	28.04	28.35	28.65	28.96	29.26	29.57	29.87	30.18
100	30.48	30.78	31.09	31.39	31.70	32.00	32.31	32.61	32.92	33.22
110	33.53	33.83	34.14	34.44	34.75	35.05	35.36	35.66	35.97	36.27
120	36.58	36.88	37.19	37.49	37.79	38.10	38.40	38.71	39.01	39.32
130	39.62	39.93	40.23	40.54	40.84	41.15	41.45	41.76	42.06	42.37
140	42.67	42.98	43.28	43.59	43.89	44.20	44.50	44.81	45.11	45.41
150	45.72	46.02	46.33	46.63	46.94	47.24	47.55	47.85	48.16	48.46
160	48.77	49.07	49.38	49.68	49.99	50.29	50.60	50.90	51.21	51.51
170	51.82	52.12	52.43	52.73	53.03	53.34	53.64	53.95	54.25	54.56
180	54.86	55.17	55.47	55.78	56.08	56.39	56.69	57.00	57.30	57.61
190	57.91	58.22	58.52	58.83	59.13	59.44	59.74	60.05	60.35	60.65
200	60.96	61.26	61.57	61.87	62.18	62.48	62.79	63.09	63.40	63.70
210	64.01	64.31	64.62	64.92	65.23	65.53	65.84	66.14	66.45	66.75
220	67,06	67.36	67.67	67.97	68.27	68.58	68.88	69.19	69.49	69.80
230	70.10	70.41	70.71	71.02	71.32	71.63	71.93	72.24	72.54	72.85
240	73.15	73.46	73.76	74.07	74.37	74.68	74.98	75.29	75.59	75.89
250	76.20	76.50	76.81	77.11	77.42	77.72	78.03	78.33	78.64	78.94
260	79.25	79.55	79.86	80.16	80.47	80.77	81.08	81.38	81.69	81.99
270	82.30	82.60	82.91	83.21	83.51	83.82	84.12	84.43	84.73	85.04
280	85.34	85.65	85.95	86.26	86.56	86.87	87.17	87.48	87.78	88.09
290	88.39	88.70	89.00	89.31	89.61	89.92	90.22	90.53	90.83	91.13
300	91.44	91.74	92.05	92.35	92.66	92.96	93.27	93.57	93.88	94.18
310	94.49	94.79	95.10	95.40	95.71	96.01	96.32	96.62	96.93	97.23
320	97.54	97.84	98.15	98.45	98.75	99.06	99.36	99.67	99.97	100.28
330	100.58	100.89	101.19	101.50	101.80	102.11	102.41	102.72	103.02	103.33
340	103.63	103.94	104.24	104.55	104.85	105.16	105.46	105.77	106.07	106.37
350	106.68	106.98	107.29	107.59	107.90	108.20	108.51	108.81	109.12	109.42
360	109.73	110.03	110.34	110.64	110.95	111.25	111.56	111.86	112.17	112.47
370	112.78	113.08	113.39	113.69	113.99	114.30	114.60	114.91	115.21	115.52
380	115.82	116.13	116.43	116.74	117.04	117.35	117.65	117.96	118.26	118.57
390	118.87	119.18	119.48	119.79	120.09	120.40	120.70	121.01	121.31	121.61
400	121.92	122.22	122.53	122.83	123.14	123.44	123.75	124.05	124.36	124.66
410	124.97	125.27	125.58	125.88	126.19	126.49	126.80	127.10	127.41	127.71
420	128.02	128.32	128.63	128.93	129.23	129.54	129.84	130.15	130.45	130.76
430	131.06	131.37	131.67	131.98	132.28	132.59	132.89	133.20	133.50	133.81
440	134.11	134.42	134.72	135.03	135.33	135.64	135.94	136.25	136.55	136.85
450	137.16	137.46	137.77	138.07	138.38	138.68	138.99	139.29	139.60	139.90
460	140.21	140.51	140.82	141.12	141.43	141.73	142.04	142.34	142.65	142.95
470	143.26	143.56	143.87	144.17	144.47	144.78	145.08	145.39	145.69	146.00
480	146.30	146.61	146.91	147.22	147.52	147.83	148.13	148.44	148.74	149.05
490	149.35	149.66	149.96	150.27	150.57	150.88	151.18	151.49	151.79	152.09
500	152.40	1,000 feet = 304.80 m; 1,500 feet = 457.20 m								

TABLE D.3. Conversion of Meters to Feet

Examples: 79 m = 259.19 feet; 230 m = 754.59 feet. 1 meter = 3.2808 feet

Meters	0	1	2	3	4	5	6	7	8	9
	Feet	Feet	Feet	Feet	Feet	Feet	Feet	Feet	Feet	Feet
0	0.00	3.28	6.56	9.84	13.12	16.40	19.68	22.97	26.25	29.53
10	32.81	36.09	39.37	42.65	45.93	49.21	52.49	55.77	59.05	62.34
20	65.62	68.90	72.18	75.46	78.74	82.02	85.30	88.58	91.86	95.14
30	98.42	101.71	104.99	108.27	111.55	114.83	118.11	121.39	124.67	127.95
40	131.23	134.51	137.79	141.08	144.36	147.64	150.92	154.20	157.48	160.76
50	164.04	167.32	170.60	173.88	177.16	180.45	183.73	187.01	190.29	193.57
60	196.85	200.13	203.41	206.69	209.97	213.25	216.53	219.82	223.10	226.38
70	229.66	232.94	236.22	239.50	242.78	246.06	249.34	252.62	255.90	259.19
80	262.47	265.75	269.03	272.31	275.59	278.87	282.15	285.43	288.71	291.99
90	295.28	298.56	301.84	305.12	308.40	311.78	314.96	318.24	321.52	324.80
100	328.08	331.36	334.65	337.93	341.21	344.49	347.77	351.05	354.33	357.61
110	360.89	364.17	367.45	370.73	374.02	377.30	380.58	383.86	387.14	390.42
120	393.70	396.98	400.26	403.54	406.82	410.10	413.39	416.67	419.95	423.23
130	426.51	429.79	433.07	436.35	439.63	442.91	446.19	449.47	452.76	456.04
140	459.32	462.60	465.88	469.16	472.44	475.72	479.00	482.28	485.56	488.84
150	492.13	495.41	498.69	501.97	505.25	508.53	511.81	515.09	518.37	521.65
160	524.93	528.21	531.50	534.78	538.06	541.34	544.62	547.90	551.18	554.46
170	557.74	561.02	564.30	567.58	570.87	574.15	577.43	580.71	583.99	587.27
180	590.55	593.83	597.11	600.39	603.67	606.95	610.24	613.52	616.80	620.08
190	623.36	626.64	629.92	633.20	636.48	639.76	643.04	646.32	649.61	652.89
200	656.17	659.45	662.73	666.01	669.29	672.57	675.85	679.13	682.41	685.70
210	688.98	692.26	695.54	698.82	702.10	705.38	708.66	711.94	715.22	718.50
220	721.78	725.07	728.35	731.63	734.91	738.19	741.47	744.75	748.03	751.31
230	754.59	757.87	761.15	764.44	767.72	771.00	774.28	777.56	780.84	784.12
240	787.40	790.68	793.96	797.24	800.52	803.81	807.09	810.37	813.65	816.93
250	820.21	823.49	826.77	830.05	833.33	836.61	839.89	843.18	846.46	849.74
260	853.02	856.30	859.58	862.86	866.14	869.42	872.70	875.98	879.26	882.55
270	885.83	899.11	892.39	895.67	898.95	902.23	905.51	908.79	912.07	915.35
280	918.63	921.92	925.20	928.48	931.76	935.04	938.32	941.60	944.88	948.16
290	951.44	954.72	958.00	961.29	964.57	967.85	971.13	974.41	977.69	980.97
300	984.25	987.53	990.81	994.09	997.37	1000.66	1003.94	1007.22	1010.50	1013.78
310	1017.06	1020.34	1023.62	1026.90	1030.18	1033.46	1036.74	1040.03	1043.31	1046.59
320	1049.87	1053.15	1056.43	1059.71	1062.99	1066.27	1069.55	1072.83	1076.12	1079.40
330	1082.68	1085.96	1089.24	1092.52	1095.80	1099.08	1102.36	1105.64	1108.92	1112.20
340	1115.49	1118.77	1122.05	1125.33	1128.61	1131.89	1135.17	1138.45	1141.73	1145.01
350	1148.29	1151.57	1154.86	1158.14	1161.42	1164.70	1167.98	1171.26	1174.54	1177.82
360	1181.10	1184.38	1187.66	1190.94	1194.23	1197.51	1200.79	1204.07	1207.35	1210.63
370	1213.91	1217.19	1220.47	1223.75	1227.03	1230.31	1233.60	1236.88	1240.16	1243.44
380	1246.72	1250.00	1253.28	1256.56	1259.84	1263.12	1266.40	1269.68	1272.97	1276.25
390	1279.53	1282.81	1286.09	1289.37	1292.65	1295.93	1299.21	1302.49	1305.77	1309.05
400	1312.34	1315.62	1318.90	1322.18	1325.46	1328.74	1332.02	1335.30	1338.58	1341.86
410	1345.14	1348.42	1351.71	1354.99	1358.27	1361.55	1364.83	1368.11	1371.39	1374.67
420	1377.95	1381.23	1384.51	1387.79	1391.08	1394.36	1397.64	1400.92	1404.20	1407.48
430	1410.76	1414.04	1417.32	1420.60	1423.88	1427.16	1430.45	1433.73	1437.01	1440.29
440	1443.57	1446.85	1450.13	1453.41	1456.69	1459.97	1463.25	1466.53	1469.82	1473.10
450	1476.38	1479.66	1482.94	1486.22	1489.50	1492.78	1496.06	1499.34	1502.62	1505.91
460	1509.19	1512.47	1515.75	1519.03	1522.31	1525.59	1528.87	1532.15	1535.43	1538.71
470	1541.99	1545.28	1548.56	1551.84	1555.12	1558.40	1561.68	1564.96	1568.24	1571.52
480	1574.80	1578.08	1581.36	1584.65	1587.93	1591.21	1594.49	1597.77	1601.05	1604.33
490	1607.61	1610.89	1614.17	1617.45	1620.73	1624.02	1627.30	1630.58	1633.86	1637.14
500	1640.42									

1,000 m = 3280.84 feet; 1,500 m = 4,921.26

TABLE D.4. Conversion of Miles to Kilometers

Examples: 107 miles = 172.20 km
380 miles = 611.55 km

1 mile = 1.6093 kilometers

Miles	0	1	2	3	4	5	6	7	8	9
	km	km	km	km	km	km	km	km	km	km
0		1.61	3.22	4.83	6.44	8.05	9.66	11.26	12.87	14.48
10	16.09	17.70	19.31	20.92	22.53	24.14	25.75	27.36	28.97	30.58
20	32.19	33.80	35.41	37.01	38.62	40.23	41.84	43.45	45.06	46.67
30	48.28	49.89	51.50	53.11	54.72	56.33	57.94	59.55	61.15	62.76
40	64.37	65.98	67.59	69.20	70.81	72.42	74.03	75.64	77.25	78.86
50	80.47	82.08	83.69	85.29	86.90	88.51	90.12	91.73	93.34	94.95
60	96.56	98.17	99.78	101.39	103.00	104.61	106.22	107.83	109.43	111.04
70	112.65	114.26	115.87	117.48	119.09	120.70	122.31	123.92	125.53	127.14
80	128.75	130.36	131.97	133.58	135.18	136.79	138.40	140.01	141.62	143.23
90	144.84	146.45	148.06	149.67	151.28	152.89	154.50	156.11	157.72	159.32
100	160.93	162.54	164.15	165.76	167.37	168.98	170.59	172.20	173.81	175.42
110	177.03	178.64	180.25	181.86	183.46	185.07	186.68	188.29	189.90	191.51
120	193.12	194.73	196.34	197.95	199.56	201.17	202.78	204.39	206.00	207.60
130	209.21	210.82	212.43	214.04	215.65	217.26	218.87	220.48	222.09	223.70
140	225.31	226.92	228.53	230.14	231.75	233.35	234.96	236.57	238.18	239.79
150	241.40	243.01	244.62	246.23	247.84	249.45	251.06	252.67	254.28	255.89
160	257.49	259.10	260.71	262.32	263.93	265.54	267.15	268.76	270.37	271.98
170	273.59	275.20	276.81	278.42	280.03	281.63	283.24	284.85	286.46	288.07
180	289.68	291.29	292.90	294.51	296.12	297.73	299.34	300.95	302.56	304.17
190	305.77	307.38	308.99	310.60	312.21	313.82	315.43	317.04	318.65	320.26
200	321.87	323.48	325.09	326.70	328.31	329.92	331.52	333.13	334.74	336.35
210	337.96	339.57	341.18	342.79	344.40	346.01	347.62	349.23	350.84	352.45
220	354.06	355.66	357.27	358.88	360.49	362.10	363.71	365.32	366.93	368.54
230	370.15	371.76	373.37	374.98	376.59	378.20	379.80	381.41	383.02	384.63
240	386.24	387.85	389.46	391.07	392.68	394.29	395.90	397.51	399.12	400.73
250	402.34	403.94	405.55	407.16	408.77	410.38	411.99	413.60	415.21	416.82
260	418.43	420.04	421.65	423.26	424.87	426.48	428.09	429.69	431.30	432.91
270	434.52	436.13	437.74	439.35	440.96	442.57	444.18	445.79	447.40	449.01
280	450.62	452.23	453.83	455.44	457.05	458.66	460.27	461.88	463.49	465.10
290	466.71	468.32	469.93	471.54	473.15	474.76	476.37	477.97	479.58	481.19
300	482.80	484.41	486.02	487.63	489.24	490.85	492.46	494.07	495.68	497.29
310	498.90	500.51	502.11	503.72	505.33	506.94	508.55	510.16	511.77	513.38
320	514.99	516.60	518.21	519.82	521.43	523.04	524.65	526.26	527.86	529.47
330	531.08	532.69	534.30	535.91	537.52	539.13	540.74	542.35	543.96	545.57
340	547.18	548.79	550.40	552.00	553.61	555.22	556.83	558.44	560.05	561.66
350	563.27	564.88	566.49	568.10	569.71	571.32	572.93	574.54	576.14	577.75
360	579.36	580.97	582.58	584.19	585.80	587.41	589.02	590.63	592.24	593.85
370	595.46	597.07	598.68	600.28	601.89	603.50	605.11	606.72	608.33	609.94
380	611.55	613.16	614.77	616.38	617.99	619.60	621.21	622.82	624.43	626.03
390	627.64	629.25	630.86	632.47	634.08	635.69	637.30	638.91	640.52	642.13
400	643.74	645.35	646.96	648.57	650.17	651.78	653.39	655.00	656.61	658.22
410	659.83	661.44	663.05	664.66	666.27	667.88	669.49	671.10	672.71	674.31
420	675.92	677.53	679.14	680.75	682.36	683.97	685.58	687.19	688.80	690.41
430	692.02	693.63	695.24	696.85	698.45	700.06	701.67	703.28	704.89	706.50
440	708.11	709.72	711.33	712.94	714.55	716.16	717.77	719.38	720.99	722.60
450	724.20	725.81	727.42	729.03	730.64	732.25	733.86	735.47	737.08	738.69
460	740.30	741.91	743.52	745.13	746.74	748.34	749.95	751.56	753.17	754.78
470	756.39	758.00	759.61	761.22	762.83	764.44	766.05	767.66	769.27	770.88
480	772.48	774.09	775.70	777.31	778.92	780.53	782.14	783.75	785.36	786.97
490	788.58	790.19	791.80	793.41	795.02	796.62	798.23	799.84	801.45	803.06
500	804.67									

1,000 miles = 1609.34 km; 1,500 miles = 2414.02 km

TABLE D.5. Conversion of Kilometers to Miles

Examples: 52 km = 32.31 miles
310 km = 192.63 miles

1 kilometer = 0.6214 mile

Kilo-meters	0	1	2	3	4	5	6	7	8	9
	miles	miles	miles	miles	miles	miles	miles	miles	miles	miles
0		0.62	1.24	1.86	2.48	3.11	3.73	4.35	4.97	5.59
10	6.21	6.83	7.46	8.08	8.70	9.32	9.94	10.56	11.18	11.81
20	12.43	13.05	13.67	14.29	14.91	15.53	16.16	16.78	17.40	18.02
30	18.64	19.26	19.88	20.50	21.13	21.75	22.37	22.99	23.61	24.23
40	24.85	25.48	26.10	26.72	27.34	27.96	28.58	29.20	29.83	30.45
50	31.07	31.69	32.31	32.93	33.55	34.17	34.80	35.42	36.04	36.66
60	37.28	37.90	38.52	39.15	39.77	40.39	41.01	41.63	42.25	42.87
70	43.50	44.12	44.74	45.36	45.98	46.60	47.22	47.85	48.47	49.09
80	49.71	50.33	50.95	51.57	52.19	52.82	53.44	54.06	54.68	55.30
90	55.92	56.54	57.17	57.79	58.41	59.03	59.65	60.27	60.89	61.52
100	62.14	62.76	63.38	64.00	64.62	65.24	65.86	66.49	67.11	67.73
110	68.35	68.97	69.59	70.21	70.84	71.46	72.08	72.70	73.32	73.94
120	74.56	75.19	75.81	76.43	77.05	77.67	78.29	78.91	79.54	80.16
130	80.78	81.40	82.02	82.64	83.26	83.88	84.51	85.13	85.75	86.37
140	86.99	87.61	88.23	88.86	89.48	90.10	90.72	91.34	91.96	92.58
150	93.21	93.83	94.45	95.07	95.69	96.31	96.93	97.56	98.18	98.80
160	99.42	100.04	100.66	101.28	101.90	102.53	103.15	103.77	104.39	105.01
170	105.63	106.25	106.88	107.50	108.12	108.74	109.36	109.98	110.60	111.22
180	111.85	112.47	113.09	113.71	114.33	114.95	115.57	116.20	116.82	117.44
190	118.06	118.68	119.30	119.92	120.55	121.17	121.79	122.41	123.03	123.65
200	124.27	124.90	125.52	126.14	126.76	127.38	128.00	128.62	129.24	129.87
210	130.49	131.11	131.73	132.35	132.97	133.59	134.22	134.84	135.46	136.08
220	136.70	137.32	137.94	138.57	139.19	139.81	140.43	141.05	141.67	142.29
230	142.91	143.54	144.16	144.78	145.40	146.02	146.64	147.26	147.89	148.51
240	149.13	149.75	150.37	150.99	151.61	152.24	152.86	153.48	154.10	154.72
250	155.34	155.96	156.58	157.21	157.83	158.45	159.07	159.69	160.31	160.93
260	161.56	162.18	162.80	163.42	164.04	164.66	165.28	165.91	166.53	167.15
270	167.77	168.39	169.01	169.63	170.26	170.88	171.50	172.12	172.74	173.36
280	173.98	174.60	175.23	175.85	176.47	177.09	177.71	178.33	178.95	179.58
290	180.20	180.82	181.44	182.06	182.68	183.30	183.93	184.55	185.17	185.79
300	186.41	187.03	187.65	188.27	188.90	189.52	190.14	190.76	191.38	192.00
310	192.63	193.25	193.87	194.49	195.11	195.73	196.35	196.97	197.60	198.22
320	198.84	199.46	200.08	200.70	201.32	201.95	202.57	203.19	203.81	204.43
330	205.05	205.67	206.29	206.92	207.54	208.16	208.78	209.40	210.02	210.64
340	211.27	211.89	212.51	213.13	213.75	214.37	214.99	215.62	216.24	216.86
350	217.48	218.10	218.72	219.34	219.96	220.59	221.21	221.83	222.45	223.07
360	223.69	224.31	224.94	225.56	226.18	226.80	227.42	228.04	228.66	229.29
370	229.91	230.53	231.15	231.77	232.39	233.01	233.64	234.26	234.89	235.50
380	236.12	236.74	237.36	237.98	238.61	239.23	239.85	240.47	241.09	241.71
390	242.33	242.96	243.58	244.20	244.82	245.44	246.06	246.68	247.31	247.93
400	248.55	249.17	249.79	250.41	251.03	251.65	252.28	252.90	253.52	254.14
410	254.76	255.38	256.00	256.63	257.25	257.87	258.49	259.11	259.73	260.35
420	260.98	261.60	262.22	262.84	263.46	264.08	264.70	265.33	265.95	266.57
430	267.19	267.81	268.43	269.05	269.67	270.30	270.92	271.54	272.16	272.78
440	273.40	274.02	274.65	275.27	275.89	276.51	277.13	277.75	278.37	279.00
450	279.62	280.24	280.86	281.48	282.10	282.72	283.34	283.97	284.59	285.21
460	285.83	286.45	287.07	287.69	288.32	288.94	289.56	290.18	290.80	291.42
470	292.04	292.67	293.29	293.91	294.53	295.15	295.77	296.39	297.01	297.64
480	298.26	298.88	299.50	300.12	300.74	301.36	301.99	302.61	303.23	303.85
490	304.47	305.09	305.71	306.34	306.96	307.58	308.20	308.82	309.44	310.06
500	310.69									

1,000 km = 621.37 miles; 1,500 km = 932.06 miles

TABLE D.6. Conversion of Fahrenheit to Centigrade and Centigrade to Fahrenheit

Examples: +23°F = -5.00°C; 99.4°F = 37.44°C; 117°F = 47.22°C; 1210°F = 654.4°C

Fahrenheit - Centigrade

- 59 to +79°F (1°F intervals)

	0	1	2	3	4	5	6	7	8	9
-50	-45.56	-46.11	-46.67	-47.22	-47.78	-48.33	-48.89	-49.44	-50.00	-50.56
-40	-40.00	-40.56	-41.11	-41.67	-42.22	-42.78	-43.33	-43.89	-44.44	-45.00
-30	-34.44	-35.00	-35.56	-36.11	-36.67	-37.22	-37.78	-38.33	-38.89	-39.44
-20	-28.89	-29.44	-30.00	-30.56	-31.11	-31.67	-32.22	-32.78	-33.33	-33.89
-10	-23.33	-23.89	-24.44	-25.00	-25.56	-26.11	-26.67	-27.22	-27.78	-28.33
-00	-17.78	-18.33	-18.89	-19.44	-20.00	-20.56	-21.11	-21.67	-22.22	-22.78
+00	-17.78	-17.22	-16.67	-16.11	-15.56	-15.00	-14.44	-13.89	-13.33	-12.78
10	-12.22	-11.67	-11.11	-10.56	-10.00	- 9.44	- 8.89	- 8.33	- 7.78	- 7.22
20	- 6.67	- 6.11	- 5.56	- 5.00	- 4.44	- 3.89	- 3.33	- 2.78	- 2.22	- 1.67
30	- 1.11	- 0.56	0.00	+ 0.56	+ 1.11	+ 1.67	+ 2.22	+ 2.78	+ 3.33	+ 3.89
40	+ 4.44	+ 5.00	+ 5.56	+ 6.11	+ 6.67	+ 7.22	+ 7.78	+ 8.33	+ 8.89	+ 9.44
50	+10.00	+10.56	+11.11	+11.67	+12.22	+12.78	+13.33	+13.89	+14.44	+15.00
60	+15.56	+16.11	+16.67	+17.22	+17.78	+18.33	+18.89	+19.44	+20.00	+20.56
70	+21.11	+21.67	+22.22	+22.78	+23.33	+23.89	+24.44	+25.00	+25.56	+26.11

80.0 to 109.9°F (1/10°F intervals)

	0	0.1	0.2	0.3	0.4	0.5	0.6	0.7	0.8	0.9
80.	26.67	26.72	26.78	26.83	26.89	26.94	27.00	27.06	27.11	27.17
81.	27.22	27.28	27.33	27.39	27.44	27.50	27.56	27.61	27.67	27.72
82.	27.78	27.83	27.89	27.94	28.00	28.06	28.11	28.17	28.22	28.28
83.	28.33	28.39	28.44	28.50	28.56	28.61	28.67	28.72	28.78	28.83
84.	28.89	28.94	29.00	29.06	29.11	29.17	29.22	29.28	29.33	29.39
85.	29.44	29.50	29.56	29.61	29.67	29.72	29.78	29.83	29.89	29.94
86.	30.00	30.06	30.11	30.17	30.22	30.28	30.33	30.39	30.44	30.50
87.	30.56	30.61	30.67	30.72	30.78	30.83	30.89	30.94	31.00	31.06
88.	31.11	31.17	31.22	31.28	31.33	31.39	31.44	31.50	31.56	31.61
89.	31.67	31.72	31.78	31.83	31.89	31.94	32.00	32.06	32.11	32.17
90.	32.22	32.28	32.33	32.39	32.44	32.50	32.56	32.61	32.67	32.72
91.	32.78	32.83	32.89	32.94	33.00	33.06	33.11	33.17	33.22	33.28
92.	33.33	33.39	33.44	33.50	33.56	33.61	33.67	33.72	33.78	33.83
93.	33.89	33.94	34.00	34.06	34.11	34.17	34.22	34.28	34.33	34.39
94.	34.44	34.50	34.56	34.61	34.67	34.72	34.78	34.83	34.89	34.94
95.	35.00	35.06	35.11	35.17	35.22	35.28	35.33	35.39	35.44	35.50
96.	35.56	35.61	35.67	35.72	35.78	35.83	35.89	35.94	36.00	36.06
97.	36.11	36.17	36.22	36.28	36.33	36.39	36.44	36.50	36.56	36.61
98.	36.67	36.72	36.78	36.83	36.89	36.94	37.00	37.06	37.11	37.17
99.	37.22	37.28	37.33	37.39	37.44	37.50	37.56	37.61	37.67	37.72
100.	37.78	37.83	37.89	37.94	38.00	38.06	38.11	38.17	38.22	38.28
101.	38.33	38.39	38.44	38.50	38.56	38.61	38.67	38.72	38.78	38.83
102.	38.89	38.94	39.00	39.06	39.11	39.17	39.22	39.28	39.33	39.39
103.	39.44	39.50	39.56	39.61	39.67	39.72	39.78	39.83	39.89	39.94
104.	40.00	40.06	40.11	40.17	40.22	40.28	40.33	40.39	40.44	40.50
105.	40.56	40.61	40.67	40.72	40.78	40.83	40.89	40.94	41.00	41.06
106.	41.11	41.17	41.22	41.28	41.33	41.39	41.44	41.50	41.56	41.61
107.	41.67	41.72	41.78	41.83	41.89	41.94	42.00	42.06	42.11	42.17
108.	42.22	42.28	42.33	42.39	42.44	42.50	42.56	42.61	42.67	42.72
109.	42.78	42.83	42.89	42.94	43.00	43.06	43.11	43.17	43.22	43.28

110 to 299°F (1°F intervals)

	0	1	2	3	4	5	6	7	8	9
110	43.33	43.89	44.44	45.00	45.56	46.11	46.67	47.22	47.78	48.33
120	48.89	49.44	50.00	50.56	51.11	51.67	52.22	52.78	53.33	53.89
130	54.44	55.00	55.56	56.11	56.67	57.22	57.78	58.33	58.89	59.44
140	60.00	60.56	61.11	61.67	62.22	62.78	63.33	63.89	64.44	65.00
150	65.56	66.11	66.67	67.22	67.78	68.33	68.89	69.44	70.00	70.56
160	71.11	71.67	72.22	72.78	73.33	73.89	74.44	75.00	75.56	76.11
170	76.67	77.22	77.78	78.33	78.89	79.44	80.00	80.56	81.11	81.67
180	82.22	82.78	83.33	83.89	84.44	85.00	85.56	86.11	86.67	87.22
190	87.78	88.33	88.89	89.44	90.00	90.56	91.11	91.67	92.22	92.78
200	93.33	93.89	94.44	95.00	95.56	96.11	96.67	97.22	97.78	98.33
210	98.89	99.44	100.0	100.6	101.1	101.7	102.2	102.8	103.3	103.9
220	104.4	105.0	105.6	106.1	106.7	107.2	107.8	108.3	108.9	109.4
230	110.0	110.6	111.1	111.7	112.2	112.8	113.3	113.9	114.4	115.0
240	115.6	116.1	116.7	117.2	117.8	118.3	118.9	119.4	120.0	120.6
250	121.1	121.7	122.2	122.8	123.3	123.9	124.4	125.0	125.6	126.1
260	126.7	127.2	127.8	128.3	128.9	129.4	130.0	130.6	131.1	131.7
270	132.2	132.8	133.3	133.9	134.4	135.0	135.6	136.1	136.7	137.2
280	137.8	138.3	138.9	139.4	140.0	140.6	141.1	141.7	142.2	142.8
290	143.3	143.9	144.4	145.0	145.6	146.1	146.7	147.2	147.8	148.3

300 to 1890°F (10°F intervals)

	0	10	20	30	40	50	60	70	80	90
300	148.9	154.4	160.0	165.6	171.1	176.7	182.2	187.8	193.3	198.9
400	204.4	210.0	215.6	221.1	226.7	232.2	237.8	243.3	248.9	254.4
500	260.0	265.6	271.1	276.7	282.2	287.8	293.3	298.9	304.4	310.0
600	315.6	321.1	326.7	332.2	337.8	343.3	348.9	354.4	360.0	365.6
700	371.1	376.7	382.2	387.8	393.3	398.9	404.4	410.0	415.6	421.1
800	426.7	432.2	437.8	443.3	448.9	454.4	460.0	465.6	471.1	476.7
900	482.2	487.8	493.3	498.9	504.4	510.0	515.6	521.1	526.7	532.2
1000	537.8	543.3	548.9	554.4	560.0	565.6	571.1	576.7	582.2	587.8
1100	593.3	598.9	604.4	610.0	615.6	621.1	626.7	632.2	637.8	643.3
1200	648.9	654.4	660.0	665.6	671.1	676.7	682.2	687.8	693.3	698.9
1300	704.4	710.0	715.6	721.1	726.7	732.2	737.8	743.3	748.9	754.4
1400	760.0	765.6	771.1	776.7	782.2	787.8	793.3	798.9	804.4	810.0
1500	815.6	821.1	826.7	832.2	837.8	843.3	848.9	854.4	860.0	865.6
1600	871.1	876.7	882.2	887.8	893.3	898.9	904.4	910.0	915.6	921.1
1700	926.7	932.2	937.8	943.3	948.9	954.4	960.0	965.6	971.1	976.7
1800	982.2	987.8	993.3	998.9	1004	1010	1016	1021	1027	1032

Examples: -14°C = +6.8°F; 38.3°C = 100.9°F; 89°C = 192.2°F; 550°C = 1022°F

Centigrade - Fahrenheit

- 59 to 0°C (1°C intervals)

	0	1	2	3	4	5	6	7	8	9
-50	-58.0	-59.8	-61.6	-63.4	-65.2	-67.0	-68.8	-70.6	-72.4	-74.2
-40	-40.0	-41.8	-43.6	-45.4	-47.2	-49.0	-50.8	-52.6	-54.4	-56.2
-30	-22.0	-23.8	-25.6	-27.4	-29.2	-31.0	-32.8	-34.6	-36.4	-38.2
-20	- 4.0	- 5.8	- 7.6	- 9.4	-11.2	-13.0	-14.8	-16.6	-18.4	-20.2
-10	+14.0	+12.2	+10.4	+ 8.6	+ 6.8	+ 5.0	+ 3.2	+ 1.4	- 0.4	- 2.2
-00	+32.0	+30.2	+28.4	+26.6	+24.8	+23.0	+21.2	+19.4	+17.6	+15.8

0 to 49.9°C (1/10°C intervals)

	0	0.1	0.2	0.3	0.4	0.5	0.6	0.7	0.8	0.9
+0.	32.00	32.18	32.36	32.54	32.72	32.90	33.08	33.26	33.44	33.62
1.	33.80	33.98	34.16	34.34	34.52	34.70	34.88	35.06	35.24	35.42
2.	35.60	35.78	35.96	36.14	36.32	36.50	36.68	36.86	37.04	37.22
3.	37.40	37.58	37.76	37.94	38.12	38.30	38.48	38.66	38.84	39.02
4.	39.20	39.38	39.56	39.74	39.92	40.10	40.28	40.46	40.64	40.82
5.	41.00	41.18	41.36	41.54	41.72	41.90	42.08	42.26	42.44	42.62
6.	42.80	42.98	43.16	43.34	43.52	43.70	43.88	44.06	44.24	44.42
7.	44.60	44.78	44.96	45.14	45.32	45.50	45.68	45.86	46.04	46.22
8.	46.40	46.58	46.76	46.94	47.12	47.30	47.48	47.66	47.84	48.02
9.	48.20	48.38	48.56	48.74	48.92	49.10	49.28	49.46	49.64	49.82
10.	50.00	50.18	50.36	50.54	50.72	50.90	51.08	51.26	51.44	51.62
11.	51.80	51.98	52.16	52.34	52.52	52.70	52.88	53.06	53.24	53.42
12.	53.60	53.78	53.96	54.14	54.32	54.50	54.68	54.86	55.04	55.22
13.	55.40	55.58	55.76	55.94	56.12	56.30	56.48	56.66	56.84	57.02
14.	57.20	57.38	57.56	57.74	57.92	58.10	58.28	58.46	58.64	58.82
15.	59.00	59.18	59.36	59.54	59.72	59.90	60.08	60.26	60.44	60.62
16.	60.80	60.98	61.16	61.34	61.52	61.70	61.88	62.06	62.24	62.42
17.	62.60	62.78	62.96	63.14	63.32	63.50	63.68	63.86	64.04	64.22
18.	64.40	64.58	64.76	64.94	65.12	65.30	65.48	65.66	65.84	66.02
19.	66.20	66.38	66.56	66.74	66.92	67.10	67.28	67.46	67.64	67.82
20.	68.00	68.18	68.36	68.54	68.72	68.90	69.08	69.26	69.44	69.62
21.	69.80	69.98	70.16	70.34	70.52	70.70	70.88	71.06	71.24	71.42
22.	71.60	71.78	71.96	72.14	72.32	72.50	72.68	72.86	73.04	73.22
23.	73.40	73.58	73.76	73.94	74.12	74.30	74.48	74.66	74.84	75.02
24.	75.20	75.38	75.56	75.74	75.92	76.10	76.28	76.46	76.64	76.82
25.	77.00	77.18	77.36	77.54	77.72	77.90	78.08	78.26	78.44	78.62
26.	78.80	78.98	79.16	79.34	79.52	79.70	79.88	80.06	80.24	80.42
27.	80.60	80.78	80.96	81.14	81.32	81.50	81.68	81.86	82.04	82.22
28.	82.40	82.58	82.76	82.94	83.12	83.30	83.48	83.66	83.84	84.02
29.	84.20	84.38	84.56	84.74	84.92	85.10	85.28	85.46	85.64	85.82
30.	86.00	86.18	86.36	86.54	86.72	86.90	87.08	87.26	87.44	87.62
31.	87.80	87.98	88.16	88.34	88.52	88.70	88.88	89.06	89.24	89.42
32.	89.60	89.78	89.96	90.14	90.32	90.50	90.68	90.86	91.04	91.22
33.	91.40	91.58	91.76	91.94	92.12	92.30	92.48	92.66	92.84	93.02
34.	93.20	93.38	93.56	93.74	93.92	94.10	94.28	94.46	94.64	94.82
35.	95.00	95.18	95.36	95.54	95.72	95.90	96.08	96.26	96.44	96.62
36.	96.80	96.98	97.16	97.34	97.52	97.70	97.88	98.06	98.24	98.42
37.	98.60	98.78	98.96	99.14	99.32	99.50	99.68	99.86	100.0	100.2
38.	100.4	100.6	100.8	100.9	101.1	101.3	101.5	101.7	101.8	102.0
39.	102.2	102.4	102.6	102.7	102.9	103.1	103.3	103.5	103.6	103.8
40.	104.0	104.2	104.4	104.5	104.7	104.9	105.1	105.3	105.4	105.6
41.	105.8	106.0	106.2	106.3	106.5	106.7	106.9	107.1	107.2	107.4
42.	107.6	107.8	108.0	108.1	108.3	108.5	108.7	108.9	109.0	109.2
43.	109.4	109.6	109.8	109.9	110.1	110.3	110.5	110.7	110.8	111.0
44.	111.2	111.4	111.6	111.7	111.9	112.1	112.3	112.5	112.6	112.8
45.	113.0	113.2	113.4	113.5	113.7	113.9	114.1	114.3	114.4	114.6
46.	114.8	115.0	115.2	115.3	115.5	115.7	115.9	116.1	116.2	116.4
47.	116.6	116.8	117.0	117.1	117.3	117.5	117.7	117.9	118.0	118.2
48.	118.4	118.6	118.8	118.9	119.1	119.3	119.5	119.7	119.8	120.0
49.	120.2	120.4	120.6	120.7	120.9	121.1	121.3	121.5	121.6	121.8

50 to 199°C (1°C intervals)

	0	1	2	3	4	5	6	7	8	9
50	122.0	123.8	125.6	127.4	129.2	131.0	132.8	134.6	136.4	138.2
60	140.0	141.8	143.6	145.4	147.2	149.0	150.8	152.6	154.4	156.2
70	158.0	159.8	161.6	163.4	165.2	167.0	168.8	170.6	172.4	174.2
80	176.0	177.8	179.6	181.4	183.2	185.0	186.8	188.6	190.4	192.2
90	194.0	195.8	197.6	199.4	201.2	203.0	204.8	206.6	208.4	210.2
100	212.0	213.8	215.6	217.4	219.2	221.0	222.8	224.6	226.4	228.2
110	230.0	231.8	233.6	235.4	237.2	239.0	240.8	242.6	244.4	246.2
120	248.0	249.8	251.6	253.4	255.2	257.0	258.8	260.6	262.4	264.2
130	266.0	267.8	269.6	271.4	273.2	275.0	276.8	278.6	280.4	282.2
140	284.0	285.8	287.6	289.4	291.2	293.0	294.8	296.6	298.4	300.2
150	302.0	303.8	305.6	307.4	309.2	311.0	312.8	314.6	316.4	318.2
160	320.0	321.8	323.6	325.4	327.2	329.0	330.8	332.6	334.4	336.2
170	338.0	339.8	341.6	343.4	345.2	347.0	348.8	350.6	352.4	354.2
180	356.0	357.8	359.6	361.4	363.2	365.0	366.8	368.6	370.4	372.2
190	374.0	375.8	377.6	379.4	381.2	383.0	384.8	386.6	388.4	390.2

100 to 990°C (10°C intervals)

	0	10	20	30	40	50	60	70	80	90
100	212	230	248	266	284	302	320	338	356	374
200	392	410	428	446	464	482	500	518	536	554
300	572	590	608	626	644	662	680	698	716	734
400	752	770	788	806	824	842	860	878	896	914
500	932	950	968	986	1004	1022	1040	1058	1076	1094
600	1112	1130	1148	1166	1184	1202	1220	1238	1256	1274
700	1292	1310	1328	1346	1364	1382	1400	1418	1436	1454
800	1472	1490	1508	1526	1544	1562	1580	1598	1616	1634
900	1652	1670	1688	1706	1724	1742	1760	1778	1796	1814

* Reproduction only by permission of the publishers of these *Scientific Tables*.

Appendix E

COMMONLY USED TERMS AND PHRASES

In certain cases, verb (v), noun (n), adverb (adv), and adjective (adj) are indicated. Numbers in parentheses refer to sections in this Guide.

aboveground (Sec. 2.13)

abrading stone

acknowledgments (Sec. 1.2.1)

aeolian
  eolian preferred

affect (Sec. 2.15.6)
  affect (v): to influence
  effect (v): to bring about
  effect (n): result, consequence

ak chin (Sec. 2.12.1)
  (farming technique)
  in italics

all over (adv): everywhere

allover (adj): covering the surface

alpha-recoil track dating
  alpha-95 value

Anasazi culture (Sec. 2.1.3)

appendix, appendixes

appliqué, appliquéd

a priori (Sec. 2.12)
  (no italics)

archaeology (Sec. 2.14)
  spell with "aeo"
  government agencies use "eo"
    (watch quotations)

archaeomagnetic dating (Sec. 2.4.2)

area (Sec. 2.1.3)
  Anasazi area

arrowshaft

ash beds

AZ BB:2:11 (Sec. 2.1.2)

AZ C:14:200 MNA (Sec. 2.1.2)

backfill

backhoe

ballcourt

barranca (Sec. 2.14)
  (no italics)

barrio (Sec. 2.14)
  (no italics)

base line

basin (Sec. 2.1.4)
  Tucson Basin

Basin-and-Range province (Sec. 2.1.3)

Basketmaker (Sec. 2.1.3)
  pre-Basketmaker is hyphenated

bear grass (Sec. 2.13)

bedrock

bighorn sheep

black-on-white (Sec. 2.2)
  Black Mesa Black-on-white
  do not use B/W

blowout

borrow pit

bottomlands

branch (Sec. 2.1.3)
  Winslow branch

brittle bush (Sec. 2.13)

brown ware (Sec. 2.2)
  Mogollon brown wares
  Verde Brown Ware

buff ware (Sec. 2.2)
  Lower Colorado buff ware
  Needles Buff

burro weed (Sec. 2.13)

bur sage (Sec. 2.13)

C-14 dates (Sec. 2.4.1)

ca., circa (Sec. 2.10)
  do not use; substitute: about

cactus, cacti (Sec. 2.15.9)

campsite

cannot
  do not use can't

canyon (Sec. 2.1.4)
  Glen Canyon

carrizo cane

cat claw (Sec. 2.13)

cattail (*Typha*)

cave (Sec. 2.1.1)
  Ventana Cave

Celsius, Centigrade (Sec. 2.7)
  18° C (82.4° F)
  use Fahrenheit equivalent in parentheses following degrees Centigrade (Table D.6)

center line

Centigrade. *See* Celsius

centiliter, cl (Sec. 2.5)

centimeter, cm (Sec. 2.5; Table D.1)

central Arizona (Sec. 2.1.4)

century (Sec. 2.6)
  first century, sixteenth century
  spell out unless frequently used
  twelfth-century artifacts

chaparral vegetation

charcoal-flecked, charcoal flecked (Sec. 2.13)
  (hyphenate if it precedes the noun)

checkdam

cheno-am

chipped stone (Sec. 2.13)
  chipped-stone tools

Christian Era (Sec. 2.1.3)

cienega

circa, ca. (Sec. 2.10)
  do not use; substitute: about

clay-lined, clay lined (Sec. 2.13)
  (hyphenate if it precedes the noun)

cliff dwelling (Sec. 2.13)
  Red Bow Cliff Dwelling
  cliff dweller

cloudblower (pipe)

Clovis-like (Sec. 2.13)

codominant

coexist

colloquium, colloquia (Sec. 2.15.9)

complex (Sec. 2.1.3)
  Llano complex

contracting-stemmed point

co-occurrence

corncob

corner-notched point

cornhusk

corrugated pottery (Sec. 2.2)
  McDonald Painted Corrugated
  Grasshopper Obliterated Corrugated
  Pine Flat Neck Corrugated
  Point of Pines Indented Corrugated

cottontail rabbit
  Nuttall's cottontail

cottonwood

courtyard

creek (Sec. 2.1.4)
  Carrizo Creek

creosote bush (Sec. 2.13)

criterion, criteria (Sec. 2.15.9)

cross-bedded (adj)

cross bedding (n)

crosscut (adj, n, v)

cross-date (v)

cross-dated (adj)

cross dating (n)

crosshatch (v)

crosshatched (adj)

cross-hatching (n)

crosspiece (n)

cross-pollinate

cross section (n)
 do not use as a verb; use section

cross-sectional (adj)

culture (Sec. 2.1.3)
 Mogollon culture

culture horizon (Sec. 2.1.3)
 Cochise culture horizon

D-shaped

data (pl)
 data are

datable

dates (Sec. 2.4)
 A.D. 1075–1200
 400 B.C. to A.D. 500
 7000–3000 B.C.
 11,000 years ago
 1920s

datum, data (Sec. 2.15.9)

desert scrub

digging stick

disk (not disc)

district (Sec. 2.1.3)
 Kayenta district

doorframe

doorsill

doorway
 T-shaped

down-cutting

downhill

downriver

downstream

draw (Sec. 2.1.4)
 Whitewater Draw

drought
 Datil Drought

dry-laid

Early Man

e.g. (Sec. 2.10)
 do not use; substitute: for example

embedded

end scraper

entryway

eolian

era (Sec. 2.1.3)
 Christian Era (by tradition)
 but: Victorian era

et al.(Sec. 2.10)
 do not use; substitute: and others

etc. (Sec. 2.10)
 do not use;
 preceding the listing, substitute: such as

ethnobotanical

extramural

farmhouse

field house

field notes

field school

fieldwork

fine-grained, fine grained (Sec 2.13)
 (hyphenate if it precedes the noun)

fire-blackened (adj)

fire cloud (n)

fire-clouded (adj)

fire-cracked (adj)

fire drill (artifact)

firepit

firewood

flaked stone (Sec. 2.13)
 flaked-stone artifacts

flint knapping

floodplain

floodwater

focus, foci (Sec. 2.15.9)

Folsom points (Sec. 2.1.3)

food gatherers

footdrum

foothill

foreshaft

foreword (Sec. 1.3.1)

forward (direction)

Four-mile Ruin

Fourmile Polychrome

freshwater snail

front-end loader

Gila monster

Gila Pueblo (GP)
  site designation (Sec. 2.1.2)
  Pearce 10:1 GP
  Sonora B:6:1 GP

Glycymeris shell (Sec. 2.9; Appendix C)

gram, g (Sec. 2.5)

grass
  bear grass (Sec. 2.13)

grassland

gray (not grey)

gray ware (Sec. 2.2)
  Tusayan Gray Ware

ground stone (Sec. 2.13)
  ground-stone artifacts

guideline

hachure (n)
  a short line used for shading

hachure (v)
  to shade with hachures

hatch (v)
  to mark with fine, closely spaced lines

Haliotis shell (Sec. 2.9; Appendix C)

hammerstone

handstone

hatchway

hearth lens

hearthstone

high-density (adj)

hilltop

historic (memorable)
  archaeological exceptions:
    historic sites
    historic period
    historic pueblos
    historic archaeology

historical (actual)
  a historical event
  (do not use an)

Hohokam culture (Sec. 2.1.3)

Hopi (Sec. 2.3)

hopper-mortar

horizon (Sec. 2.1.3)
  Culiacan horizon

house
  farmhouse
  field house
  pit house (two words)
  house mound

i.e. (Sec. 2.10)
  do not use;
  substitute: that is

imbedded
  use: embedded

index, indexes
  (plural is indices in statistics)

infer, inferred (v)

inference (n)

in situ (Sec. 2.12)
  (no italics)

inter, interred (v)

interment (n)

interbedded

island (Sec. 2.1.4)
  San Juan Island

jackrabbit (Webster)
  antelope jackrabbit

jar rest

judgment

Kayenta district (Sec. 2.1.3)

kill site (Sec. 2.1.3)
  Lehner Ranch Kill Site

kilogram, kg (Sec. 2.5)

kilometer, km (Sec. 2.5)
  (Conversion tables in Appendix D)

LA 847 (Sec. 2.1.2)
  Laboratory of Anthropology site designation

landform

lapstone

large-scale (adj)

lean-to (n)

lens (not lense)
  lenses (pl)
  hearth lens

life zone
  Canadian life zone
  Upper Sonoran life zone

liter, l (Sec. 2.5)

lithic scatter (n)

lithic-scatter sites (adj)

locus, loci (Sec. 2.15.9)

long-term (adj)

low-density (adj)

low-lying (adj)

macrobotanical

manuscript
  spell out in text
  MS (singular)
  MSS (plural)

marshland

masonry-lined

mesa (Sec. 2.1.4)
  Paiute Mesa

mealing bin

meter, m (Sec. 2.5)
  (Conversion tables in Appendix D)

microenvironment

middle Gila (Sec. 2.1.4)

mid-June (Sec. 2.4)

midpoint

millennium
  first millennium B.C.

milling stone

Mogollon culture (Sec. 2.1.3)

Mohs' scale

mollusk (n), molluscan (adj)

mortar hole

mound
  house mound
  platform mound
  Mound 8

mountains (Sec. 2.1.4)
  Santa Catalina Mountains

mudstone

multicomponent (adj)

multistage (adj), but multiple-stage

multistoried building

museum
  Arizona State Museum
    (for subsequent references in text, use the Museum or ASM; check with editor)

Museum of Northern Arizona
  (MNA)

NA 11,047 (Sec. 2.1.2)
  Museum of Northern Arizona site designation

Navajo (Sec. 2.3)
  not Navaho

neck-banded jar (Sec. 2.2)
  Alma Neck Banded

needlelike

nether stones

nonarchitectural

nonceramic

nondomesticates

Olivella shell (Sec. 2.9; Appendix C)

overhang

overlie
  x overlies y
  x overlying y
  x overlay y (*past* tense only)
  y was overlain by 2 m of debris
    Do not mix these verb forms with the verb "to overlay"

pack rat

paho, pahos
  (no italics)

paleoclimate

paleoecology

Paleo-Indian

palo verde (Sec. 2.13)

Papago (Sec. 2.15)
  do not use, except in quotations
  substitute: Tohono O'odham

Papaguería

Parry agave (Sec. 2.9; Appendix A)
  Agave parryi

Pecten shell (Sec. 2.9; Appendix C)

pendant (n)

pendent (adj)

percent (Sec. 2.8)

percussion-flaked, percussion flaked
  (hyphenate if it precedes the noun)

period (Sec. 2.1.3)
  Pioneer period

phase (Sec. 2.1.3)
  Sacaton phase

phenomenon, phenomena (Sec. 2.15.9)

Pima (Sec. 2.3)

Pimería Alta

pinyon

pit house (two words)

pit oven

pit structure

plain ware (Sec. 2.2)

plateau (Sec. 2.1.4)
  Colorado Plateau

platform mound

pochteca (Sec. 2.12)
  in italics first time used only

podcorn

point
  projectile point preferred
  but: Clovis point

polishing stone

ponderosa pine (Sec. 2.9)

post–1941 (Sec. 2.4)

postglacial

posthole

post-Pleistocene

postpluvial

pot cover

pot hunter

potrest

potsherd

pottery (Sec. 2.2)
  Southwestern
    Alma Plain (not Plainware)
    Mesa Verde Black-on-white
    Tusayan Corrugated: Tusayan Variety
    Grasshopper Obliterated Corrugated
    Rincon Red
    Tularosa Fillet Rim
    Mogollon brown wares (general)
    red ware sherds
    Hohokam buff wares
    plain ware
    do *not* adjoin the word "ware" to pottery type names
  Mesoamerican
    Yalbac Smudged-brown
    Urita Gouged-incised

preagricultural

pre-Basketmaker

precede, preceding

preceramic

pre-Classic (in the Southwest; Sec. 2.13)
  but: Preclassic Maya

Precolumbian (Sec. 2.13)

predate

pre-Hispanic (Sec. 2.13)

pre-Pueblo (Sec. 2.13)

pressure-flaked, pressure flaked
  (hyphenate if it precedes the noun)

prickly pear

projectile, projectiles (do not use)
  projectile point preferred
  but: Clovis point
    Folsom fluted point

pronghorn antelope

proto-Hispanic

protohistoric

protopalette

protopestle

prototype

Provo Pluvial

Pueblo people

pueblo (Sec. 2.1.1)
  Starkweather Pueblo

ranchería (Sec. 2.12)
  in italics first time used only

radiocarbon (Sec. 2.4.1)

reconstructible (not reconstructable)

red-on-brown (Sec. 2.2)
  Tanque Verde Red-on-brown

red ware (Sec. 2.2)
  White Mountain Red Ware

reevaluate

reexamine

region (Sec. 2.1.3)
  Maya region

reorientation

reservation
  Zuni Reservation

reuse

ridge (Sec. 2.1.1)
  Nantack Ridge

ridgetop

right-of-way

river (Sec. 2.1.4)
  Colorado River
  Gila and Salt rivers

riverbed

river bottom

rock-filled
  (hyphenate if it precedes the noun)

rock shelter

roof fall

room block

root (Sec. 2.1.3)
  Patayan root

rubbing stone

ruin (Sec. 2.1.1)
  Hodges Ruin

runoff

sagebrush

saguaro
  (not sahuaro)

saltbush

Salt-Gila expedition

sandstone

sand temper
  (but: sand-tempered plain ware)

savanna
  (not savannah)

seed beater

semiarid (Sec. 2.13)

seminomadic (Sec. 2.13)

semipermanent (Sec. 2.13)

semisedentary (Sec. 2.13)

Seri (Sec. 2.3)

shaft smoother

sheetwash

shell (Sec. 2.9; Appendix C)
  Glycymeris
  Olivella

sherd temper
  sherd-tempered pottery

Show Low (town)

Showlow Polychrome

side scraper

sipapu, sipapus

site names (Sec. 2.1.1)
  Naco Site
  SU Site
  a Trincheras site (nonspecific)
  a Pine Lawn phase site

site numbers (Sec. 2.1.2)
  AZ BB:2:11 ASM
  AZ C:14:200 MNA
  LA 847
  NA 11,047

site survey files

slash-and-burn

sociocultural

socioeconomic

socioenvironmental

socioreligious

Sonora B:6:1 GP (Sec. 2.1.2)
  Gila Pueblo site designation

southwest (Sec. 2.1.4)
  direction

Southwest (Sec. 2.1.4)
  specific term signifying a particular culture area
  Southwestern Indians

Spanish Conquest
  the Conquest

spindle whorl

stage (Sec. 2.1.3)
  San Pedro stage

stairway

stratagem

strategy

stratum, strata (Sec. 2.15.9)

SU Site

sub-age

subdominant

subfeatures

subfloor

subpluvial

subrectangular

subsurface

symposium, symposia (Sec. 2.15.9)

tableland

three-quarter grooved

Tohono O'odham (Sec. 2.15)
  use in place of Papago, except in quotations

tradition (Sec. 2.1.3)
  Anasazi tradition

trash-filled (adj)

trash mound

tree-ring dating

Turritella shell (Sec. 2.9; Appendix C)

two-story pueblo

usable

U.S.G.S.

valley (Sec. 2.1.4)
  Santa Cruz Valley
  but: the Rio Sonora valley

variety, ceramic (Sec. 2.2)
  Tusayan Corrugated: Tusayan Variety

village (Sec. 2.1.3)
  Cave Creek Village
  Promontory Village
  Hohokam villages

ware (Sec. 2.2)
  brown ware
  buff ware
  gray ware
  plain ware
  red ware
  trade ware
  white ware
  Cibola White Ware
  White Mountain Red Ware

wash (Sec. 2.1.4)
  Cow Springs Wash

watercourse

water table

waterworn (Sec. 2.13)

wattle-and-daub
  synonym: jacal

white ware (Sec. 2.2)

wickerwork

woodland

woodrat

yucca
  narrow-leafed yucca

zone
  life zone

Zuni (Sec. 2.3)